WHAT PEOPLE ARE SAYING

"Joe Jordan's engaging stories will help any advisor deepen their sense of meaning and purpose. *Living a Life of Significance* is a gift to help boost energy, confidence, and clarity, teaching advisors how their work creates profound transformations in countless lives."

Dan Sullivan
Founder of Strategic Coach®

"This book is a must-read. All organizations and individuals must have strong values. Joe Jordan focuses on these values. Although he talks about financial services, he is really talking about life."

Jack Keane
Retired Four-Star General & Former Vice Chief of Staff of the U.S. Army

"Joe's philosophy became self-evident as he understood how certain financial tools would have changed his family's life. He has an air of wisdom, empathy, and renaissance. All the best, my friend."

Phil Harriman
Former Million Dollar Round Table (MDRT) President

"*Living a Life of Significance* is essential reading for your practice and for your soul."

Nick Murray
"Resources" in Nick Murray Interactive, July 2011

"There are only a handful of people who go about their everyday lives working to make a difference, and Joe is one of them. A life of significance is something we all must choose to do, and Joe supplies the motivation."

Gordon Watson

Executive Vice President & Regional Managing Director, AIA Group

"Jordan is an Olympic-sized thinker who motivates and inspires in a manner that is without peer. Your practice has been short-changed if you haven't read every word."

Dr. Larry Barton, CAP®

President and CEO, The American College

"Joe is an inspirational speaker who cares passionately about the financial profession and fully understands the challenges these experts face."

Fay Goddard, UK

Chief Executive of The Personal Finance Society

*See full text of **What People Are Saying** on page 171 in the back of the book.

Living a Life of
SIGNIFICANCE
Second Edition

By Joseph W. Jordan

FOREWORD BY
ROBERT BENMOSCHE

Published By Acanthus Publishing - 2013

Published by Acanthus Publishing, Boston, Massachusetts.

*Chief Seattle speech used with permission from Ted Perry, Fletcher Professor of the
Arts and Professor of Film & Media Culture

Reference herein to any commercial product, service, or company/organization by
trade name, trademark, service mark, or other promotional language/imagery does not
constitute or imply an endorsement or recommendation by Joseph Jordan. The purpose
of this promotional material, which appears on the back cover, is to encourage use of
the book and concepts within certain companies/organizations. In all dealings with the
insurance and financial services industries, Joseph Jordan remains impartial and does
not endorse a particular company, product, or service.

Dedication

Jordan Family Motto:
"Percussus Resurgo"

To my mother, Marie Williams Jordan, whose grace, dignity, and sense of humor in adversity taught me life's most valuable lesson.

Table of Contents

ACKNOWLEDGEMENTS

I would like to express my sincere appreciation to my wife, Geraldine; my daughter, Sarah; and my son, Joey, for their encouragement.

I would also like to recognize the contributions of the outstanding staff at Acanthus Publishing. For Paige Stover Hague's assistance with this book, the editorial skills of Madeline Rau, Theresa Yannetty, and Andrea Weidknecht, and the design work of Ian Nichols and Billi Solis.

Gratitude goes to those who shared their stories in this book: Jack Dempsey, T.J. Rogers, Ann Marie Miller, Art Steinberg, Bob Weaver, Paris Lewis, Lonnie Colson, Mike Amine, Ying Ling Zhang, Roland Basinski, David McBride, Kathy McBride, and the Cobb family.

I want to thank Thia Reggio, who helped write the book. In addition, I would like to show my appreciation for Nick Murray — both for his wisdom and example, and for introducing me to Steven Pressfield's book *The War of Art*, which pushed me to finish this book. I am also grateful to Bob Benmosche for his support, along with Larry Barton and Eileen McDonnell, who proposed the idea of writing this book. I very much appreciate Jack Turner for getting me started. And a special thanks to Joel L. Franks, whose dedication and perseverance made this book possible.

FOREWORD

Joseph Jordan is a gifted communicator with a deep knowledge of insurance products, their construction, and pricing. Though these qualities place him among a select group of colleagues, these are not his most extraordinary capabilities.

The most compelling quality that separates Joe from the other members of this select group is his ability to perceive financial products in the greater scheme of things and think about them from the perspective of our customers, rather than how industry insiders see them.

Joe Jordan's constitution is built on a strong set of personal values. He possesses an internal set of ethical guidelines that enable him to look at the insurance industry from a distinct perspective. From Joe's view of the world, we in the insurance industry earn our living in the noblest profession on earth, and each one of us is living a life of significance. I cannot imagine a better way to define the mission of the organization I have the great honor to lead.

Joe discusses how the "Longevity Tsunami"[1] is overwhelming traditional benefits and entitlements of governments and corporations. He sheds light on the subject; he explains how the insurance industry is uniquely positioned to provide independence, dignity, and legacy to the aging population of the world. This mission should

---

[1] "Australia's Longevity Tsunami – What Should We Do?" Actuaries Institute WHITE PAPER, August 2012.

be the major message of our industry: inspiring financial professionals to think beyond personal gain and to focus on the impact we have on individuals. As traditional entitlements are disappearing, this should be our time for financial services professionals to rise up. We must regain the trust required to help people overcome today's dramatic changes.

A man who has mastered the complexity of simplicity, Joe urges us not to focus on *what* we want (corporate, personal goals) and *how* to get what we want (knowledge, skills, strategy), but *why* we do it. Evaluating our mission to focus on living a life of significance in the service of others inspires us to overcome any obstacle. Viktor Frankl, a Nazi concentration camp survivor, once said, "He who has a *why* to live can bear almost any *how*." All of us who have made our career in the financial service industry owe a debt of gratitude to Joe Jordan for restoring our collective self-esteem at a time when we are most needed.

Share this book with your professional colleagues. Help support the movement to restore the public image of the insurance industry. It all starts with us, with you. By incorporating the ideas Joe Jordan offers in this book, we can transform society's perception of us and regain our sense of purpose.

Read this book and pass it on. The faster we can achieve momentum in this reawakening movement, the sooner we can breathe a collective sigh of relief. I applaud the role Joe Jordan has taken to become the "Ambassador of Significance" for the industry. His message strikes the core of everything we do. I petition you to join me and take the pledge to Live a Life of Significance™. The greatest beneficiary of this new paradigm is you.

Yours in Significance,
Bob Benmosche
CEO & President, AIG
New York, NY
February 2013

INTRODUCTION

THE NOBLEST PROFESSION IN THE WORLD

If you are in the financial services business or contemplating becoming a financial services professional, you should know that it is the noblest profession on earth. You will not read this in the press or hear it from any television commentary, but it is true. The insurance industry deals with the defining issue of the 21st century—not energy, global warming, or terrorism—it is the aging population of the world.

Human beings have never lived this long. Did you know that by 2062 there will be five nations—China, India, the United States, Indonesia, and Brazil—that have at least 50 million people over 60 years old? And that this group will be growing five times faster than any other cohort.

Japan will lose 18% of its population in the next 50 years and is projected to lose half of its current population by the end of the 21st century.[2] In 2008, Japan bought more adult diapers than baby diapers. All schools built there have ramps and handrails for when the babies disappear. It is incredibly worrisome that 97% of the world's population now lives in countries where the fertility rate is dropping dramatically.[3]

---

[2] Jeff Wheelwright, "Gray Tsunami," *Discover Magazine*, October 2012, 32.

[3] Jonathan V. Last, *What to Expect When No One's Expecting: America's Coming Demographic Disaster* (New York City: Encounter Books, 2013).

DECLINE OF ENTITLEMENTS

In the February 5, 2013, issue of the *Wall Street Journal*, Gerald Seib stated in his article, "Hidden Secrets of Spending," that "Government, particularly at the federal level, is turning increasingly into an entitlement machine, dispensing benefits to those who qualify, while a combination of recession, deficits, and an aversion to new taxes is squeezing most remaining government activity."[4]

On a global level, governments, companies, and centuries-old cultural practices of caring for senior citizens are breaking down. The end result is that people are on their own.

10,000 PEOPLE A DAY

In the United States alone, 10,000 people a day for the next 10 years will be retiring with their life savings. They need to turn their assets into a lifestyle-sustaining income for the rest of their lives, but most are ill-equipped and confused as to how to do this. Never has there been a more desperate need for financial professionals to help people assume the responsibility of self-reliance.

The insurance, or protection industry is uniquely positioned to deal with this issue. Originally, the business was founded on the premise of protecting people from dying too soon. Now it can provide people with independence and dignity while living longer.

[4] Gerald Seib, "Hidden Secrets of Spending," *The Wall Street Journal*, February 2013, A4.

LIFE OF SIGNIFICANCE

This book celebrates the intrinsic value of the financial services professional. Intrinsic value is not measured by how much money you make, but by the size of the problem you can solve. The insurance industry offers financial services dealing with the major human issues of our time:

1. Keeping a business or family going in the event of premature death

2. Offering a retirement income that cannot be outlived — providing *independence*

3. Protecting that income if someone becomes sick or disabled — preserving *dignity*

4. Providing a *legacy* when people die

These are the human issues of our time and what the business of financial services is all about. Our job is about the people we serve. Not just how you can enrich yourself, but how you can fulfill yourself. As an industry, we need to become more vocal about the impact we have on our clients. Contained in this book are several examples of how the lives of clients and financial services professionals are impacted. Also included is my own personal journey of almost 40 years in the business. After experiencing so many dramatic changes, it took me more than three decades to discover what this business is all about: it's not about us, but the people we serve.

This book will rekindle for those in financial services the purpose and passion lost through day to day frustrations. But more importantly, this is for those that are just starting out.

We spend a lot of time in our business focusing on *what* we want; these are our desires and goals. We also spend much time worrying about *how* to get what we want—with skills and knowledge. But we never spend enough time answering *why* we are participating in this business. If the *why* you do it is because you want to make a lot of money, you can succeed, sure. But in my opinion, it will be a very difficult career.

If all you care about is money, your work life— and, your personal life—will likely be unrewarding and layered with negativity. Over time, you will eventually become ground down with bouts of self-pity and a fear of prospecting. At best, you will make money and feel unhappy. At worst, you will fail. However, if you are in the business to provide critically needed help to those who have been abandoned by governments and corporations, you will live a life of significance. By helping people enjoy independence and dignity in their lives, your career will be blessed with enrichment and fulfillment. It won't be easy, but it will be infinitely more rewarding than just doing it for the money.

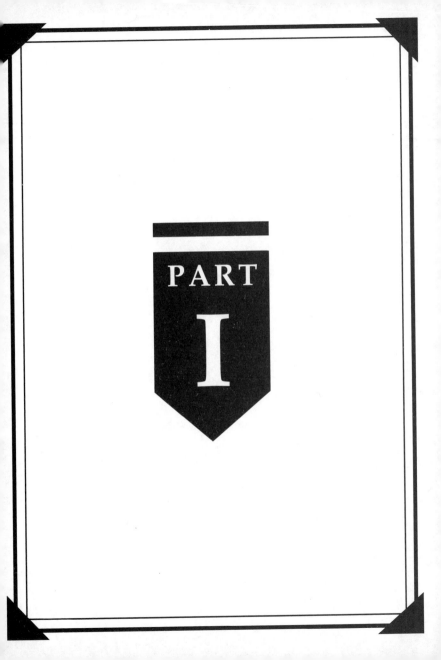

PART

I

CHAPTER 1

Do You Hear What I Hear?

"The important thing is not to stop questioning. Curiosity has its own reason for existing. One cannot help but be in awe when one contemplates the mysteries of eternity, of life, of the marvelous structure of reality. It is enough if one tries merely to comprehend a little of this mystery every day. Never lose a holy curiosity."

— ALBERT EINSTEIN

The nature of our society seems to advocate against questioning our choices in life, particularly those made in our professional lives. We worry that interrogating past decisions may indicate a sign of weakness. Worse, we fear where these questions might actually lead us. But in all reality, we are in good company when we question. If I can help one person see the value of that "holy curiosity" Einstein spoke of, I will have shared a valuable lesson.

To inspire the practice of questioning, you'll find prompts dispersed throughout the book to offset the text.

As I write the second edition of this book, the global economy is still reeling from Wall Street's 2008 crisis and individuals are trying to put their lives back together following devastating losses in the financial market. Let us recast the challenges of today and draw more deeply from the reservoirs of accumulated knowledge. Patterns of human behavior and natural law reach back into the past and continue to shape history far into the future. Identifying patterns in your own life can help you cultivate the skills to ensure that your own personal narrative will reveal a life of significance.

In the early 1990s, I joined MetLife after almost a decade on Wall Street. At the time, brokers and insurance agents were operating in two distinct cultures, with two different approaches to their clients. I was coming from PaineWebber's asset-gathering broker culture. My function at MetLife was to focus on building its annuity business. That business existed under the influence of protection-focused life insurance agents whose principal objective was to gather income. Looking back, I suspect that I was hired because of my extensive knowledge of the product. From my perspective, my best asset was my understanding that in the context of industry culture, human behavior has everything to do with the sales process. Conscious that the brokerage and insurance industries had distinctive attributes, I found that I did not need to train people on a product but to alter their behavior.

In the investment world, brokers focus on accumulation of assets in investment portfolios. Depending on the broker and the client, the amount of a single transaction may vary greatly. If a client has a million dollars in assets to invest, a broker is interested in bringing as much of that million under management as possible. Having been in the life insurance business, I knew that life insurance people for the most part gathered income for protection purposes. They never asked for a million dollars up front. In terms of behavior, that was the fundamental difference between the two.

What was not discussed in the 1990s was the fact that all financial products are on some level tied to human needs and desires. For me, the key was to find the correlation between the cultures that ruled Wall Street and those that fueled the insurance industry, and then leverage both to the advantage of the protection product marketplace.

In my early years at MetLife, we recognized that the best approach to insurance-related asset gathering was to become a viable provider of financial planning services. Fee-based financial planning had been emerging for some time, as traditional barriers between brokerage, banking, and credit were lifted by legislation and a more fluid financial services industry was born. In this fluid environment, an institution like MetLife, with traditional roots in insurance products, had an increased capacity to provide a wide range of products and services to its clients. The creation of a financial planning model would allow us to aggregate those products and services with regard to a client's personalized plan. A design of this capacity would not happen overnight.

A few years after starting at MetLife, a nagging question plagued me: Why isn't the financial planning business soaring? All in all, things were going well. Then in its infancy, our financial planning approach at MetLife was gaining momentum; sales figures were good. It was the height of the Information Age, and our "information" was giving us a pretty optimistic picture. Something was holding everyone—both planners and clients—back from maximizing the full potential of the process. I began to speculate whether there was something wrong with the process itself. I would soon come to realize that this was not the issue.

By that time, I had spent 25 years in the financial industry, and I'd seen many changes. I had been on the insurance side of the investment business and the investment side of the insurance business. I charted my career as an "outlier,"[5] as I always liked coming from the outside into a new situation. I enjoyed bringing skills or experience from another industry into the mix. As a result, I possessed a fairly unique perspective on the changes in finance that took place in the final third of the 20th century.

From the client perspective, I wondered, "If people are armed with the information they need to plan a solid financial future, then why are they slow to put the plan into action?" I knew that financial planning made inherently good sense. Our clients understood the value of a plan, at least to the extent that they would purchase the plan itself. But they were not as engaged when it came to following advice the plan laid out for them.

[5] Malcolm Gladwell, *Outliers: The Story of Success* (New York City: Little, Brown and Company, 2008).

From the planner's perspective, I questioned what was preventing clients from embracing the planning model wholeheartedly. This is why I wondered if the process itself needed fixing. Much later I discovered that these two questions were tied to a common denominator: *behavior*.

CHAPTER 2

That Time Before

"Intellectual awareness and knowledge of something motivates us to do nothing."

— DAVID HUME

When I took the leap into the insurance business in 1974 at a small company called Phoenix Home Life (which no longer exists), everyone was selling products that had been around for years. The products were whole life and term life. It is important to remember that in the 1970s, insurance, banking, credit, and investing operated separately from one another. Most working Americans, if they had anything they called a "retirement" account, would have had a pension or some other defined benefit plan for retirement. Many people (more men than women in those days) also had some form of traditional life insurance. There was no motivation to design updated insurance products at that time.

As the '70s gave way to the '80s, however, America faced record inflation and an oil crisis, compounded by the hostage crisis in Iran. Americans felt vulnerable. Products such as life insurance policies that relied on cash values with fixed interest rates—even healthy ones—suddenly seemed doomed to be outpaced by inflation. Interestingly, history shows that the majority of the whole life policies held by policyholders through that time period performed well.

By the early '80s, it seemed inevitable that the new restructurings in place would ultimately break down the dividing walls of the separate types of financial institutions. By the mid-'80s, defined benefit plans (like the pensions mentioned above) had been largely replaced by defined contribution plans. Most working people had a 401(k) and market-based investments. These were once the pursuit of sophisticated institutional investors; they had now reached a new and largely uninitiated audience of "investors." Everyone from the proverbial kid in the mailroom to the CEO in the executive suite had a more immediate stake in the markets.

The allure of the investment culture was compelling. "Choice" and "control" were the bywords of the day. Rather than using traditional savings accounts, people began to perceive personal investing as a way to not only increase their chances of earning higher returns on their money, but also to gain hands-on control of how their assets were allocated.

The appeal of a defined benefit plan was the security of knowing the amount you would receive in retirement. The appeal of the defined contribution plan was the potential to earn more by controlling the underlying investments directly. With inflation threatening to diminish future dollar values, the marketing story of the defined contribution was quite effective. From the perspective of the employer, the appeal was in shifting the fiscal responsibility onto employees and alleviating a growing financial burden for what would ultimately be America's largest group of retirees: the baby boomers.

A powerful current swept people toward Wall Street, and the appeal of investing gripped the public. This type of career called to the big crop of 20-somethings with the business training and energy to pursue their goals. Along with two friends, I dove into the trendy end of the financial services pool and joined a boutique investment firm as the resident insurance expert.

At the time, the product at the intersection of investing and insurance was annuity. Like most products at the time, annuities were fairly straightforward in their design. As a guaranteed income vehicle, a vanilla annuity product could be described as upside-down life insurance. While life insurance (funded by those who lived longer) paid benefits for those who died prematurely based on a mortality pool, annuities (funded by people who died earlier) paid income for those who lived longer into retirement age.

However, the design premise and the sales strategy did not always match. Brokerage firms were selling annuities as tax-deferred investments. With interest rates hovering around 15% and equities at a low ebb, brokers took notice. Brokers quickly discovered that their clients could take money out on a FIFO (first in, first out) basis. There, annuities were being sold like 10-year tax-free municipal bonds. Since they were allowed to withdraw at least 10% of their investment each year, they would have tax-free income for the first 10 years (At the time, annuities allowed people to withdraw basis or principle first. Later this was changed to LIFO—last in, first out—making the withdrawal taxable).

I discovered another interesting wrinkle. For the most part, the annuity products our company was selling came from small, lesser-known insurance companies. These companies could offer high interest rates because they were not carrying the huge bond portfolios that the big insurers had backing their existing policies at the time. Large, established life insurance companies also had a protection income-gathering culture and, consequently, were late to enter this use of annuities. On the insurance side of the aisle, the need to update insurance products became increasingly pressing.

The questions I focus on today are the same as those that tugged at me early in my career: What would help people make the right choices for their lifetime and for the generations to follow them? I understood the value of an insurance policy or an annuity when purchased with the proper goals in mind. Even then, as I watched the way the protection benefit of the annuity was being downplayed and disregarded in the sales conversation, I had questions not about the products, but about how they were being sold. When you force a product to perform in a way other than it was designed to perform, what new risks are you introducing? It seemed to me that no one was looking at the products holistically.

Not everyone on Wall Street in the '80s had this vision in mind. I'm sure I couldn't have articulated the relevance of my questions at the time, either. But I came to realize that when products are bought and sold for reasons other than those for which they were structured, problems ensue. Even in my thirties I did not feel comfortable with this practice. However, I did not yet have the benefit of experience that could help me detect the source of my uneasiness.

When **John Moran**, who had taken the plunge into the Wall Street waters with me, notified me that PaineWebber was looking for someone to run the insurance department, I was eager for a chance to move on. I was not immune to the stigma that insurance agents were feeling during this period. I wanted to alter my image. Initially, I was completely intimidated at the prospect of heading a department. But when John said, "Joe, just go to the interview," I went.

When have you done something despite feeling intimidated?

I went into that interview feeling both less and more qualified than I actually may have been. Before the interview began, I had no way of knowing what I might be asked. But as the questions came, my confidence rose. I realized that, despite the interviewer's seniority, I had expertise that he did not possess.

"Tell me about Section 264." Something in the way he presented the question hinted that I knew more than he did about how to answer.

"That is the minimum deposit requirement that allows the efficient purchase of life insurance by paying the first four years of the seven-year premium up front." You see, the policy that PaineWebber had in mind was a high cash value, low death benefit plan. For example, a premium of $10,000 gave you an initial death benefit of $14,000 after which you paid four out of seven years and then borrowed the full cash value out while continuing to deduct interest. Future premium payments were paid by loans that were tax-deductible, offset by tax-free withdrawals of excess cash from the policies. The result was predictable, multiple write-offs.

You might wonder who would buy a $14,000 life insurance policy for $10,000. At that time, there was no standardized definition of life insurance. Creative minds set out to construct products that, if considered life insurance, assured considerable tax benefits. This was not insurance; this was a tax shelter. The tax advantages life insurance enjoyed were being manipulated as a social good. When the deductibility of interest and the proper definition of life insurance were finally legislated, this system died.

I could see that my answer had struck a chord. The next question came swiftly. "Can you do this job?"

"Of course I can," I heard myself saying. And somewhere inside I knew that I could…or, I might fail…but it was a risk worth taking.

"Then it's yours."

Imagine that! I came home and told my wife I got the job. The pay was $60,000 a year, plus a $25,000 guaranteed bonus.

The national sales manager for insurance products at PaineWebber is responsible for introducing insurance products to 4,300 brokers. I gave my notice to John Moran, and he wished me luck. My wife helped me pick out a couple of new suits. Then I rolled up my sleeves and went to work.

My top priority was to get acquainted with all the brokers and all the suppliers who worked with us. It meant a grueling travel schedule and long hours, but I learned a great deal in short order, including the ins and outs of booking airline tickets and filing travel expenses. Everything was new to me—except for the products.

In 1981, after seven years of straight commissions, Geraldine said, "We never have to worry about money again." We had hit the big time.

I had come to PaineWebber primarily because I wanted to stay current. But PaineWebber also gave me the opportunity to be affiliated with a substantial and reputable firm. The firm's prestige was reassuring both to clients and to those of us working there in a time of rapid-fire changes. The markets and products were evolving quickly. The demand for returns and performance drove everything the insurance companies designed. I had an instinct that there would need to be a broader context for investors to remain secure. To achieve this, I worked with brokers to make them more comfortable selling annuities, since they would be able to gauge how these products would fit into a client's portfolio. At the same time, I worked to involve life insurance experts in selling investments, again providing a broader perspective on how products would fit into the larger financial picture for a client.

Of course no one wanted to be identified as a life insurance agent. Everyone who wasn't a registered broker fancied a title like "financial advisor" or "investment representative." It took years for me to recognize the discomfort this raised in me at the time. I knew it was unhealthy for people to feel they had to hide their profession. But, at the time, I didn't consider the additional layer of confusion this attitude added to a market where products were being sold as something other than what they were intended to be. I was years away from realizing how this basic self-esteem issue could affect sales overall.

Another phenomenon of this era was the junk bond. Michael Milken built a junk bond empire on the illusion created by massive liquidity, high coupon rates, and timing. People were swindled into enjoying these bonds without realizing the high risk of their underlying investments. Ultimately, of course, the illusion was dispelled, the junk bonds collapsed, and Milken went to jail for fraud.

An article in 1992 about a company called Executive Life, which appeared in *Fortune* and on CNN.com, highlighted the issues that were affecting the less stable parts of the insurance industry in some of its early attempts to sell protection products based on performance numbers. The essence of the story was that grabbing for growth with insufficient assets to underwrite the risk caused outside auditors to sound the alarm. It was a poisonous cocktail for

Executive Life's Fred Carr and his investors.

From my position at PaineWebber, I could see the changes happening before my eyes. The bellwether case of undercapitalized annuity risk was Baldwin-United, which was mentioned in the same article. Baldwin's story unfolded in the early '80s, illustrating the pitfalls that lay in the path of products and companies manipulated for "unnatural purposes." Baldwin was a successful piano company run by Morley Thompson. Thompson was inspired by the creation of corporate conglomerates. Regardless of its traditional focus, a company could acquire businesses across industries to realize profits from a number of sectors.

Thompson decided to parlay his piano company into a multifaceted financial services business. He acquired small insurance companies and began offering annuity products. Unencumbered by large low interest rate bond portfolios and offering double-digit interest rates packaged within the supposed safety of an insurance company, the plan was initially successful.

Thompson's fatal error was to invest the money Baldwin-United was raising with these products in "affiliated assets." Essentially all the money was being funneled back into building the corporation in order to continue building the conglomerate. Actuarial firms and rating agencies were not equipped to assess the security of these types of muddled corporate structures. Eventually, rumors began flying that Baldwin-United was unstable. When the tremors reached those of us in the brokerage community, there was a range of reactions.

A colleague at another Wall Street firm divulged that he was going to advise his clients to take out half of the funds in their Baldwin-United annuities. To which I shot back, "Which half? The good half or the bad half?" No one wanted to create a run on the bank. But my own internal conversation was bubbling over; I was bursting with anxiety. I cornered everyone—at home, with family and friends—anywhere I could get someone to listen to my babbling about insurance commissioners and actuarial assessments. People started to dread the headline or random comment that would send me off on these "inside baseball" conversations.

In the midst of this storm brewing, PaineWebber flew me to Club Med for a brokers' meeting. It was my first trip to an island resort. But from the moment I stepped off the plane and caught a glimpse of the crystal waters and white sand beaches, I somehow knew that I would not be able to enjoy myself.

Sure enough, the storm broke both literally and figuratively. As dark clouds rolled in from the ocean and rain began streaming down the veranda, word came from New York that the Arkansas insurance commissioner had closed the door on Baldwin-United. All annuity assets were frozen.

After nearly coming to blows with an unnaturally calm concierge who felt it was his mission to pacify uptight New Yorkers, I finally got through to my office and booked a flight home (this was the era before cell phones). I would not be a part of a PaineWebber headline titled, "Big Shots on the Beach," while our clients might be losing their life savings. On the flight home, I started strategizing. The goal was to assess the potential loss, formulate our response, and calm brokers and policyholders across the country. No small task, but it had to be done.

Back in the office, I began working with my staff and the branches to set up town hall meetings, one region at a time. We brought together groups of clients, sometimes as many as 500 in one room. The insurance regulators devised a plan that would allow us to return the annuity assets at a substantially lower interest rate, and clients had to wait three and a half years to get their money. We held the meetings and listened to the heated venting, but the minute they heard they were going to get their money back, the fury subsided. And with each encounter, I grew another inch of steel in my backbone. We were not on Wall Street anymore; these were real people putting their faith in Wall Street. Their candor reminded me of a Mark Twain quote, "Don't tell me about the return on my money, tell me about the return of it." And thankfully, we were able to do just that. We informed people that their money would be returned, with interest.

With this experience I learned an important lesson: Security is the most important thing to those who buy a guaranteed product. Unlike the savings and loan fiasco that would follow in a few short years and cost the tax-payers a fortune, the life insurance industry was able to absorb the cost of repaying investors in the wake of this disaster.

As part of PaineWebber's reorganization following Baldwin-United, I reported to the new sheriff in town: Bob Benmosche. Bob was hired to lead the company's competitive efforts to match Merrill Lynch's nascent Cash Management Account (CMA). The CMA was a game-changing vehicle that brought brokerage and banking together in a new way, providing an incentive for clients to consolidate their assets with a single firm. Despite skepticism in the brokerage community, CMA proved to be the "killer app" of financial services in the 1980s.

After the re-org, I was initially concerned that I would lose my job despite the positive resolution I had helped devise for our annuity clients. But Bob was observant and a shrewd businessman. He noticed the due diligence books on my desk. He asked me what I saw there. When I told him that one of our annuity carriers had some issues that made me uncomfortable, he reviewed the material for himself.

"We will stop sales from this company immediately," he resolved.

I agreed with his conclusion, but I felt duty-bound to explain to him that the head of the company in question was a tour de force on Wall Street, and a personal friend of our own company's president. I will never forget the events that followed.

We called this titan of Wall Street in for a meeting. The confidence I had quickly left me. Upon walking out of the elevator, he grabbed my hand to shake it and said, "Hi Joe, how are you?" My legs immediately turned to jelly. I asked him in a shaky voice if he wanted coffee. We went into the meeting room and he began to speak with a dominating presence. He made a persuasive argument about de-emphasizing his product line, and I found myself nodding in favor of doing just that. Heck, I would have believed him if he took credit for oxygen. I was thoroughly intimidated. The room fell silent, and everyone there seemed to think he'd made his point.

Bob Benmosche broke the silence with, "Let me tell you why the answer is NO." I was taken aback by the abruptness of his statement. Bob explained that we had to stop sales in light of the Baldwin-United collapse, because, unless we took a proactive stand, our brokers would discount us. Bob then added, "This is the right thing to do now, for all of us and especially our policyholders."

The forcefulness of his statement reminded me of Butch Cassidy and the Sundance Kid. In the movie, Paul Newman kept repeating, "Who is that guy?" in reference to an Indian named Lord Baltimore who, despite all their tricks to cover their tracks, kept following Butch and Sundance.

I wondered, "Who is this guy?" Who can make a point abundantly clear against all the nodding heads in the room? Since Bob had done all the heavy lifting, my confidence returned. I walked boastfully as I escorted the titan and his entourage to the elevator.

When I returned to my desk, the phone was already ringing. It was Don Nickelson, president of PaineWebber.

He said, "Joe, I have [Mr. X] in my office. He tells me you are stopping sales. Do we have to do this now?"

All the confidence I'd had moments before drained from my body. "Maybe not," I stuttered. "I'll talk to Bob."

I found Bob and sheepishly told him Don Nickelson called to ask if we had to take this action now. Bob looked at me and asked, "So what did you tell him?" I began stammering once again. He glared at me and said, "Come with me."

We arrived in the executive suite — Oz, we called it — and were announced. Nickelson rose behind his desk and motioned to the chairs opposite him. As we sat, Bob began, referring to me. "This young man found trouble here. We can't sell these products. Sales need to stop immediately, right, Joe?"

With such a forceful ally, I could only speak with integrity. "That's what the due diligence tells me," I said bashfully.

"So, unless you want to run the goddamn insurance department, we're going to do as he says," Bob said sternly. Once again I thought to myself, "Who is this guy?"

"All right, then," Nickelson answered.

What I did not know at the time was that Don Nickelson was Bob Benmosche's mentor. He was challenging us to see if we had strength in our convictions. Ironically, I have seen Bob use this tactic many times on others: challenging people to see how strongly they believed in a certain course of action. Essentially, if you came back at him forcefully, he would back you.

This was a great lesson in leadership for me. Bob had the courage to not be intimidated by people, he made a shrewd business decision, and he backed his subordinate. He was not testing for a rational solution; he was testing for passion, emotion.

Bob Benmosche had taught me to stick to my guns. But perhaps more importantly, he had been a role model for teamwork and mentoring young people. After all, I knew that Bob had been hired in part to help keep our noses clean. He could have taken credit for the discovery. Strictly speaking, he did not need me in any of those meetings. But he saw the value in presenting a united front, and he wasn't afraid to acknowledge another person's contribution.

After retiring from MetLife, Bob became CEO of AIG. At the time, the company was the poster child for the financial meltdown of 2008. The previous chairman who had attempted to save the company was trying to show good faith—he agreed to be paid $1 a year for the job. There is a saying that "no good deed goes unpunished." Congress turned him into a punching bag, and rather than help, they used his visits to Congress for political grandstanding. When Bob took the job, he insisted he should be paid for his efforts. He also halted all efforts to dismantle the company. Many experts today feel that if AIG had been broken up and sold in its entirety at fire sale prices, it would never have been able to pay off the $182 billion the government had put up to stabilize AIG.

Bob immediately went on a whirlwind tour to meet as many employees of AIG as he could. He told everyone that they were the real victims, they had done an excellent job, and that they truly lived a life of significance. Together, they would revitalize the company. He did just that. After a number of intelligent business decisions and the selling of selective parts of AIG, Bob not only paid back the $182 billion, but also gave the government a profit of $22 billion. Talk about leadership.

Additionally, I think we should salute the senior management of AIG, who stayed and kept the company going and partnered with Bob Benmosche when he arrived to help execute this remarkable turnaround. We should also recognize **Hank Greenberg**, the former chairman and CEO of AIG, also laid a remarkable foundation for the company, as it was able to recover under Benmosche's stewardship.

Jay Fishman, chairman and CEO of Travelers, appeared on the Charlie Rose television show in February 2013. In discussing how critical leadership is, Fishman said, "Employees will always try to do what leadership tells them to do." Leadership is responsible for framing the focus and purpose of an organization. Speaking about Benmosche, Fishman said, "Benmosche is a hero! How do you hold people together to get the human capital to stay engaged and feel good about what they do? Bob Benmosche made smart business decisions, but whatever he did from the human capital side is remarkable!"

There is a difference between management and leadership. Much of management deals with rational thinking. While important, as Kevin Roberts of Saatchi & Saatchi says, "Rational thinking leads to conclusions, and conclusions do not solve problems. Emotions do because they lead to action." Leadership needs to inspire people to action. It is crucial to let people know that they are doing something worthwhile. Given the Longevity Tsunami and the collapse of corporate and governmental entitlements, the role of the insurance business is fundamental. When leadership forgets its purpose, bad things happen.

Jay Fishman mentioned that AIG rented out their credit rating prior to the crisis. He said this had never even occured to him because he understood his organization's purpose. He felt it was an insurance company and he managed it accordingly. While companies need to make money in the long run, they need to do it within the framework of why they exist. At the end of the day, they have to figure out what human needs they satisfy. When they only pursue short-term quarterly goals, they lose their purpose, and once that happens, no amount of inspired leadership or management can help. It is a good thing we have people like Bob Benmosche and Jay Fishman.

CHAPTER 3

Dawn of The Information Age

Acolleague of mine named **Mike Farrell** made an astute observation about the connection between technology and financial services. He pointed to the 1980s — when the PC was introduced — as the watershed moment for the data-driven mindset in finance. Conceptual discussions about policy benefits were replaced by illustrations and spreadsheets virtually overnight. Adding the financial catalyst for the perfect storm, interest rates were hovering around 14%. This put more pressure on product development to revisit traditional insurance and investment products. By the '90s people were bombarded with choices. These choices were not only in finance; they surfaced at every level. Annuities and universal life products with a host of fixed and variable rate structures flowed into the mix with equities, options, bonds, and REITs, or Real Estate Investment Trusts. Now people had to choose how to allocate investments, even if it was only through an employer's retirement plan. The average person was ill-equipped to make any of the choices intelligently because they lacked the expertise to guide them. As people began to express their need for information, personal computer technology found a receptive audience.

The '80s and '90s put computers in the spotlight, bringing them into offices and homes across America. Spreadsheets that had once only churned out of huge backroom operations now danced on desktop screens in kitchens and office cubicles alike. It was the information revolution we had been waiting for. Like most in the financial services industry, I wanted to believe that if people just had the right information, they would make the right choices.

I could see the double-edged sword of an increasing focus on statistics, charts, and other "clinical" data. All the attention was on performance and numbers.

Just a few years earlier I had turned to MetLife, exploring the possibility of applying my experience in the brokerage environment to an insurance company. MetLife was appealing because it was a company I had come to respect for the reliability of its product offerings and because I felt the need to come home to the insurance business. Once again, I had followed my personal need for security to a company where I felt that the security of the client was a top priority.

When has a choice for personal fulfillment or security in your own life been tied to the security of others?

I had helped institute financial planning at MetLife, and it was succeeding to a point. But I still felt something was missing from the sales equation in our financial planning process. More information was just reinforcing the mistaken impression that what mattered was numbers. I couldn't yet bring it to fruition, but I knew it had to be about the people. It was about the stories, the lives and legacies, and the generations that are affected by the numbers on a page. We were concentrating on communication when what we needed was a connection. The clues were hidden in the faces of those relieved annuity clients whose faith in a sound investment had been validated. There were clues in the missteps of Baldwin-United and within my own story.

In that moment I was looking at charts and graphs, wrestling with the message that our reps were taking out into the field. Now that people had all this information at their fingertips, did they really have what they needed to make sound financial choices? Was this information giving them an advantage, or just paralyzing them with data?

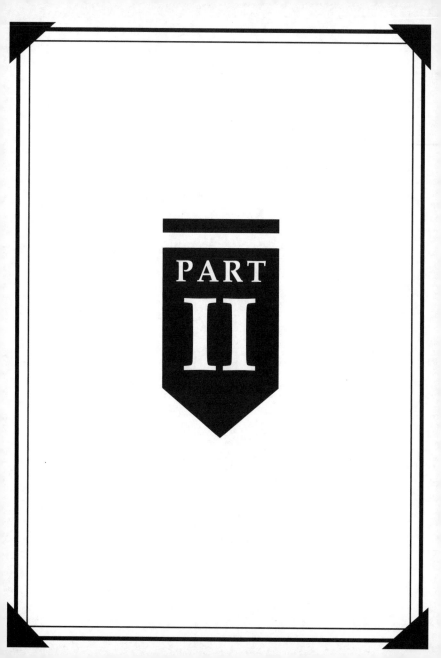

PART

II

CHAPTER 4

Important Influences

"Computers [and their data] are like Old Testament gods; lots of rules and no mercy."

— JOSEPH CAMPBELL

Considering the patterns in our lives, Joseph Campbell provides some interesting food for thought. In his masterwork, *The Hero's Journey*, Campbell points out similar themes that are shared among all great folklore and myths around the world. Across the widest range of cultures, stories tell of a hero who passes through milestones that are remarkably similar in sequence and significance. Campbell was clear that the earliest moments in a person's life initiate the shaping process that will ultimately reveal interconnected patterns among the seeming randomness of our lives. Our earliest influences—parents, siblings, teachers—contribute to our conscious and subconscious choices. I had no stronger influence than my mother.

All heroes, it seems, undergo a transformative encounter with a wise mentor (think Yoda in *Star Wars*) who gives the hero a "sacred gift" that instills a power in him he had not previously known. I might call this memory that came back to me my Yoda moment:

One night I was visiting my alma mater, Fordham University, when I spotted an old friend and former teacher named **Father Rushmore**. Although I didn't realize it at the time, this was a particularly important reunion for me, and certainly not one I had on my calendar. As we caught up on mutual acquaintances and discussed the unseasonably nice weather, my friend asked me what I was up to professionally. I told him that I had recently started working at MetLife. He asked me if I enjoyed my work. I was happy that I could tell him I did. Then he asked if I ever wondered whether I had made the right choice in my career. At the time the question caught me up short. *I'm not really an introspective guy*, I thought.

"Why do you ask?"

His answer surprised me. "Not a day goes by when I don't consider my choices and challenge myself about my vocation," he said flatly. "I ask myself tough questions because I have taken on a big responsibility in this life. I feel that I owe it to the people who count on me."

In that moment, my old friend opened a door for me. I didn't walk through it right away, but I saw the little slit of light ahead of me. He was saying that questioning and challenging yourself is healthy and imperative, and it has the potential to make you better at what you do.

It may even help you understand why you do what you do.

> *What questions do you have about your career path?*
>
> *Do you sense any tension between who you are and what you do?*

I had to smile. "But Father, you're 87 years old," I chuckled. "Don't you think you ought to have it down by now?"

"Ah," he replied, looking over his spectacles right into my soul. "You don't remember the quote I used in my class? A life unexamined isn't worth living."

Not everyone follows the same paths in life. We aren't all priests, and we aren't all outliers. But we can all take valuable lessons from the journeys of others. Father Rushmore affirmed for me the importance of questioning for the sake of it, and I didn't even fathom that I was looking for this affirmation. From there, I began to notice the voices of many others who saw the benefit of questioning. So, I embraced it. I read and watched and heard the questions.

I began to see that I was doing something with my life that I could feel good about. Joseph Campbell would call it "following your bliss." But I hadn't made the connection yet between the personal and the professional implications of all I was learning. From a business perspective, I still did not know why it was right. I hadn't yet reconciled everything I saw going on around me with my personal sense of wellbeing. Nevertheless, I turned a corner and began a new phase of my life in which the questions became my allies. One big question had been answered, and a lifetime of prosperous questioning had begun.

Before I had made the connection between Father Rushmore's counsel and the situation at hand with the MetLife financial planning practice, I had already started to apply the same hungry curiosity to exploring expert perspectives on the financial industry.

In the next few pages, I'll introduce some of those who influenced my thought process and helped me evaluate my priorities for financial planning. **Nick Murray**, a prominent financial author, gave me valuable information about behavioral economics. It was Murray who opened my eyes to what had troubled me with data-based sales theories. He presented without a single graph or chart. Instead, he focused on investor behavior and the emotions that motivated people. It was as though I heard the first tumbler click into place, unlocking a new way to connect with clients.

Nick Murray's emphasis on behavioral economics focuses on the premise that people make bad financial decisions based on emotional reactions, such as euphoria and panic. Murray suggests that a paradigm of "selection and timing"[6] has put both financial professionals and clients into a performance derby that is impossible to win simply

---

[6] Nick Murray, *Behavioral Investment Counseling* (Southold, NY: The Nick Murray Company, 2008).

because it is not a goal. He states that financial professionals should focus on managing client behavior rather than performance.

Csaba Sziklai is a psychologist and the founder of the Advocacy System. He explores self-esteem issues among his clients, many of whom have come from the insurance industry. Sziklai stresses the importance of positive reinforcement and relationship building in client interactions. This connects to the humanity of the interaction and not the transaction that it triggers. Sziklai's core message is built around the importance of being an advocate, especially for those who may not have a voice in a financial decision. It is for the ones who will be deeply affected by its outcome: husbands, wives, children, and business partners.

Sziklai had a revelation about life in the insurance business. He observed that many insurance professionals were not publicly honest about what they did for a living. Some were embarrassed about being part of the insurance business and, as a result, appeared insincere to clients and even to themselves.

In a strange parallel, we encounter many clients who are in denial of their own mortality. Sziklai's Advocacy System builds scripts to reinforce that the work of an insurance professional is something to be proud of, not ashamed of.

Daniel Pink, with his groundbreaking analysis on the relevance of right-brain (emotional) and left-brain (analytical) thought, allowed me to put my own perspective on the context of our evolving culture. I came to believe that my lifelong discomfort with performance-based investing and investing by the numbers tied in perfectly with the emerging opinions of the day. Intuition, the purview of the stepchild "right brain," demands equal attention as we refine our approach to providing financial services. **Dan Ariely**, an economist who asserted the importance of emotion specifically as it applies to economic theory, declared "The End of Rational Economics" in the *Harvard Business Review*.[7] I agree with Daniel Pink when he suggests that we need a "Whole New Mind"[8] as we move into the heart of the 21st century, where intellect may actually take a back seat to intuition.

Here were experts from different fields — psychology, economics, and sociology — with a common thread that became increasingly obvious to me: Intuition and emotion are central to all human decisions and interactions.

My focus in the financial arena has always been to find ways to protect individuals for the long term. Taking a lifelong viewpoint with people comes naturally when you have a relationship with them.

Insurance products are designed to take care of human needs. I like to say that the insurance business humanizes the capital markets by paying people money when they need it most. The left-brain calculates the odds of dying young and discounts the need for life insurance. The decision to buy life insurance should not be determined by math, but by the

---

[7] Dan Ariely, "The End of Rational Economics," *Harvard Business Review*, July–August 2009, 78-84.

[8] Daniel Pink, *A Whole New Mind: Why Right-Brainers Will Rule the Future* (New York City: Riverhead Trade, 2005).

consequences of the decision. What are the consequences if you get sick, die young, or outlive your money?

First, you have to insure what can go wrong to gain the luxury to invest in what can go right. These decisions are not the domain of the analytical mind, but of the emotional, behavioral mind. Consequently, it was not difficult for me to embrace the wisdom of tapping into intuitive urges as part of a strategy for financial planning.

CHAPTER 5

Stories That Resonate

The following stories tie back into one underlying truth: You can make a difference in the life of another person.

With Love, from China

A longtime agent and financial planner named **Jack Dempsey** shared a story of a young woman who did her financial planning from the heart.

> My client—we'll call her Sally—contacted my office to discuss insurance for her small business, a Christmas tree farm. I invited her into my office to meet face-to-face. As we talked about the right policy for her business, I asked her about her retirement plan. She had none. "Well, your employer really ought to provide a retirement plan," I joked. In all seriousness, I explained that at her young age of 30, retirement savings would accumulate over her lifetime. As a self-employed person, she would have to consider things that another employer would otherwise do for her. After she set money aside for

retirement, Sally agreed and chose a $100,000 universal life plan with her mother as the beneficiary. Sally told me that she wanted to be sure her mom was taken care of if anything happened to her, because her dad had failed to do so. When he died at a young age, her mom was thrown back into the workforce as a school cook in order to support herself and her two young daughters.

Sally was still in her early thirties when she called me again. She had found herself in a position to purchase her aunt's Christmas decoration shop as a complement to her successful tree farm. She had entered an installment plan with her aunt for a purchase price of $160,000. She wanted to be sure that it was paid, if for any reason she was unable to make the payments. So, we covered the business with annual convertible term. I delivered the policy that Wednesday.

On that Saturday, Sally was killed in a car crash. Her mother received the $100,000, which she placed in an annuity that allowed her to retire and draw a comfortable income. I delivered the $160,000 to Sally's aunt, who was in poor health and able to cover her care with the proceeds.

But the story doesn't end there. Due to her aunt's poor health, Sally's sister Diane inherited the business. A few years later I was reviewing the business insurance with Diane, when she shared with me another chapter in Sally's life. Because of Sally's careful planning, Diane had inherited the business debt-free. She and her husband had never been able to have children, nor had they had the financial resources to pay for costly fertility or adoption alternatives. But with the business free, clear, and successfully up and running because of Sally, Diane and her husband could afford to adopt a beautiful little girl from China. They named her Sally.

As I listened to Diane that day, I realized that the "insurance proceeds" I delivered on her behalf were really love letters. The letter to her mother said, "I want to make sure you can retire, Mom. You deserve it, and I want to give that gift to you." The letter to her aunt read, "I know you can't afford to have me drop the ball with these payments. You've worked hard for your business. I honor that commitment and I want to make sure that I live up to my word." And the love letter to Diane said, "I trust you with the businesses that were such a huge part of my life, but I don't want to saddle you with a financial burden that will just make things harder." But the letter that Sally didn't even know she wrote was to her niece and namesake. That letter read, "Welcome to the family. You will never know me, but I live on through you."

Getting Priorities Straight

In this story from a Financial Advisor, **T.J. Rogers** highlights the importance of advocacy.

> *On September 10, 2001, my wife and I were spending a romantic week in Paris. We planned to return the following week to get our children back to school. That night, we had a beautiful black tie dinner in a beautiful restaurant. The next day was September 11 — THE September 11 — and back home in New York all hell broke loose. Travel restrictions kept us in France for another five days before we could return home.*
>
> *Being separated from our children was the hardest part for us. They were eight and nine at the time. The next morning when phone service was restored, we called them. My daughter got on the phone and said that her best friend's father was on one of the airplanes that hit the buildings. Though I didn't know him well, this was a person I saw almost every day dropping off and picking up his kids from school. Like so many New Yorkers, I had that "there but for the grace of God" feeling. It was a real-life nightmare.*
>
> *A couple of days after our return, we had the little girl to a sleepover with our daughter. I invited her mom to breakfast the next morning. While we sat at the breakfast table, I offered my assistance with any issues related to her husband's death. I explained I was in the insurance business and assured her that I would be happy to help her with any claims issues or anything*

else she needed. At this point she opened up about his situation and what he had for life insurance – which was, apparently, not much. She said she had to think about what she was going to do next and what kind of job she was going to get. She had to decide whether or not to sell the house since it needed work.

As she spoke I pictured her late husband in the schoolyard. This was a person I would look at and think, "He'd be a nice guy to have as a client." But it was one of those situations where it's easy to talk yourself out of starting a conversation. You think to yourself, "I don't want to approach somebody in the schoolyard...the timing just isn't right." Well, I never approached him. And I was now stuck wondering, "What if..." If I had talked to him about his planning, maybe he would have purchased some insurance from me since he was inadequately covered. If he'd spent $50 a month on a million of term, both his wife's and daughter's lives would have dramatically changed for the better. The moral of the story is: Don't put yourself in a situation where something like this happens and you regret not making that phone call.

I didn't cross the schoolyard. Maybe I was afraid of the rejection. I used to put my pride first. Now when I see these kids trooping into school, I put them first. Now the parents of my children's friends are at the top of my list to discuss financial planning with. It isn't a difficult conversation now that I lived through the story of that little girl and her mom. I just picture the little girl and my commitment swallows up my pride.

A Father's Story

A story from MetLife financial advisor **Ann Marie Miller** illustrates this kind of connection to a deep, intuitive wisdom on both the part of the financial advisor and her client. Ann Marie incorporated the gift from a father to a son to open up a conversation that neither client nor advisor could have known would become so significant. A father's love for his son, a son's love for his mother, and the woman who shed light on the significance of both — this is the story of Ann Marie Miller.

Ann Marie got a call one day from a client who wanted to cancel a policy. It was understandable; it was a baby policy on this young man who was now in his early twenties. Ann Marie told the young man that she would like to meet him and discuss the cancellation.

"This policy was a gift to you from your father," she reminded him.

A simple reminder that his father had valued his son's life set the stage for a conversation in which the young man realized how life insurance can make a difference. Even though he was a young man and unmarried, he bought a policy from Ann Marie that day. He did this to take care of his mother, who was relying solely on Social Security.

When he married, Ann Marie helped him insure his wife. As his children were born, she wrote policies for each of them. She made sure her client had sufficient coverage as his income and responsibilities increased.

One day, the young man's wife called to tell Ann Marie that he had passed away. Ann Marie cannot tell this part of the story without tears in her eyes. As the family sat around the kitchen table, the emotion was overwhelming. The young man's mother repeated in Italian, "My son, my son."

Ann Marie recalls, "To my surprise, all they kept saying to me was, 'What would we be doing now without you?' And I thought, 'I had no idea that what I had done was so significant.'"

The legacy of a father's love, translated by this caring woman and her wise young client, became the saving grace for a new generation and solace for a mother's loss.

Notice Ann Marie said she did not realize how significant her actions were. This is the part of the business that needs more emphasis and exposure. If you have not experienced something similar to Ann Marie's story, borrow her experience.

CHAPTER 6

View From the Future

A s I investigated outside sources that might help me enhance MetLife's approach, I was prompted to revisit the events in my own life that might hold hidden insights. My intuition told me that some of the answers to my professional questions might be rooted in my personal history.

A new century was on the horizon. Given all that happened in the first decade of the new millennium, it seems trivial from where we sit now, but the huge concern at the time was Y2K. Programmers everywhere were fixated on the possibility that databases would be erased wholesale when the internal settings displayed double zeroes in the year fields. Since their inception, computers had been programmed using a two-digit system for month, day, and year (MM/DD/YY instead of MM/DD/YYYY). As the year 2000 approached, programmers went into a frenzy to prevent the catastrophe that might occur when the zeroes rolled over like lemons on a cosmic slot machine. Would programs erase themselves on a cue that this was the year "00," signaling a start-over mode? It was no joke. Financial systems, government systems, medical systems — everything faced the same exposure. But 2000 arrived, and the threat of crisis passed.

The press, and particularly the financial press, loves to highlight the crisis de jour. They feed the aberrant behavior that many investors manifest (euphoria at the top and panic at the bottom). This would be reaffirmed during the tech and subprime mortgage bubbles, which we experienced in the first decade of the century.

Although very few escaped unscathed in 2008 and 2009, we were insulated at MetLife from both the tech markets and the subprime mortgages. Prior to the 2000s, my attention had been on the crucial question of how to fully realize the concept of financial planning. This question seemed to have led to the very solutions that helped our clients weather the financial storm of those years.

Yes, I still had my concerns about Y2K. And thanks to my refreshed memory of Father Rushmore and his wisdom about intellectual curiosity, I was reveling in questions instead of pushing them aside. With the new millennium just over the horizon, I found myself on the road in a hotel room down in Florida. I had just checked into my room a few hours prior to a meeting. I turned on the TV to view a public service announcement (PSA):

> An elderly woman sits looking out through a lace-curtained window. As the camera pans back, there is a bustle of movers emptying the room. A younger woman escorts the elderly woman to a car. The old woman doesn't say a word, but a voice-over expresses her thoughts.

> "I know what's going on here, I wish you'd just say it.
> You don't really want me to live with you.
> Your house really is too small and I'm sure the money's tight.
> Besides--I'm his mother, not yours.
> You probably think this isn't your responsibility.
> Yes, I can see it on your face.
> You wish someone else was stuck with me.
> That would be more convenient for you, wouldn't it."

As I stared at the screen, in my mind's eye, I saw my wife and my mother playing out a scene from fifteen years earlier. I sank into the bed, absorbing what I'd just observed. I had never considered how my mother felt about moving in with us. I hadn't considered how it affected her dignity, or even whether she questioned our willingness to have her with us.

I discovered that the line between my personal and my professional choices was an illusion. In the coming years, I would replay that PSA in my head over and over to explore the reaction it evoked in me. There was a reason I had persevered in the insurance business, and it had as much to do with my sense of morals as it did with my professional ambition or, frankly, any rational decision I'd ever made.

CHAPTER 7

A Life Interrupted

"He is a poor son whose sonship does not make him desire to serve all men's mothers."

— HARRY EMERSON FOSDICK

Harry Fosdick, a key figure in an early twentieth century movement called the Social Gospel, understood that a parent's great joy is found in a child who serves the greater good. My career, especially my years at MetLife, have allowed me to do just that. I hoped this would make me a better son in the eyes of my mother.

From as far back as I can remember, I looked up to my mother. She was the person I most admired and whose admiration meant the most to me. In these past few years, I have learned much about my relationship with my mother and now recognize that the things I do for others — particularly those in need of an advocate — are the things that would make my mother most proud.

At the age of 40, my mother — a woman who'd had tea at the White House (my father had been an advisor to President Truman) and enjoyed a life of relative prosperity — found herself widowed with four small children. I was the youngest, at nine months old when my father passed. It was 1952 and single mothers were certainly not the norm. But the worst blow, after losing my father, came on the day my mother learned that he'd cashed in his life insurance policy just a few days before his death. A widow with four children, my mother had no financial cushion. She would have to work.

Without missing a beat, my mother put on a pair of crisp white gloves, her best hat, and landed a job as a secretary for the local bartenders union. She worked 40 hours a week to keep us clothed, fed, and in our home in the Bronx. She was known as the duchess of the neighborhood in decades to come for her regal bearing and impeccable sense of style. My mother was a trailblazer. She rose to the occasion that fate had handed her, and never let on to us that there was any other way to live.

Years later, on that night in Florida, I gazed back at my path through life. I remembered how proud I was of my mother and the way she took care of us. As a child, I didn't realize that things could have been different if we'd had a financial safety net. Despite my mother's best efforts, certain parts of the situation did become clear. After my father's death, we were unmistakably deemed the poor relatives. We couldn't afford a car to visit my cousins. We had to take the train or the bus in order to have a holiday or vacation. But my relatives would never stoop to visit us in the Bronx, and that sort of thing registers with a kid. There was also the fact that our stylish clothes weren't quite so stylish by the time my mother permitted us to buy something new. In junior high, I grasped that we were just a little out of step. In the end, all I needed to know was that if my mother could work that hard, I could too.

At 13, I got my first job working at the neighborhood dry cleaner. I worked six days a week during the summer and on weekends over the school year. I contributed what I could, and eventually I worked my way through college. However, the toughest decision my mother had to make was not allowing my two sisters to go to college at the normal age, even though one of them had received a full scholarship. They had to go to work to make sure the "boys" (my older brother and I) could go to college. How do you like that legacy? Today, as I write this — in November 2013 — I am 61 years old. And the impact that decision had on my sisters still has ramifications today.

I think I made my family proud when I got into Fordham University. I was serious about making the most of college. I wasn't a big kid physically, but I was determined and strong. I made the football team my freshman year, playing offensive guard. It was a position that called for relentless single-mindedness. I didn't look left or right once a play was called; I headed straight into the guy in front of me. Most of those guys were a head taller than I was, but that didn't stop me. I had a job to do and I did it. I guess I did it pretty well because, despite my size, I was named All East in 1971 and 1972, and later I was inducted into the Fordham Athletic Hall of Fame. I also played rugby at Fordham, a sport that ultimately led me to forge relationships that still exist today. And then there were the jobs.

In the summer of 1971, one of my neighbors in the construction trade sponsored me to work with the New York Iron Workers. In the union vernacular, he was my rabbi. The pay was great—$7 an hour—so I went for it. This time it wasn't my height that was an issue; it was my paralyzing fear of heights. I had to balance up to 700 feet above the ground, and for a few days, I was on top of the World Trade Center. Trembling on a steel beam about two feet wide, I spent my summer in complete denial.

Despite my fear, it was a great experience to meet all the different characters that worked the high steel. My first building was the Fisher Tower on 45th Street and 6th Avenue. When I got to the site, I looked up and saw a building with 44 stories. The first 34 stories had full floors; the next 10 were just red steel. They put me on the hoist and sent me up. You may have noticed, when passing a construction site, that there is an elevator shaft on the outside of the building. It is designed to send up building materials such as concrete and sheet rock. It has no sides and it moves tremendously fast. The next thing I knew, I was rocketing up to the 34th floor. Ascending to the 44th floor required going up an open staircase.

Right at the edge of the building, there was nothing but red steel, clouds, and birds. I kept thinking about Led Zeppelin's hit, "Stairway to Heaven." I was absolutely terrified. I met the crew and they could see how scared I was. They went out of their way to help me cope with the fear. It was clear that they were proud of their craft and were real professionals.

One crew member was a pretty famous actor, who at the time was going through a dry spell in his career. He would tell me things about Hollywood actors—most of which is known today—but seemed scandalous to my young ears in 1971.

Then there was Duke. Duke was about 5'8", thinly built, and always wore sunglasses and black pointy shoes complimented by an all-white outfit. He clearly didn't want to risk losing his sartorial splendor to a pair of rubber-soled boots. He had a pack of non-filtered cigarettes rolled up in the sleeve of his t-shirt. He was right out of a James Dean movie, and despite his choice in shoes, a real artisan on the steel. He moved like a cat, but he also liked to showboat. He would wrap his legs around a beam and hang upside down, waving to the secretaries in the Time-Life building.

Marty was the foreman. Marty was a big, red-faced, gregarious guy. He spoke loudly all the time and had the curious habit of never uttering a sentence without an expletive. I always wondered if he greeted his wife, "Honey, how the **** are you?" Duke and Marty used to like to give each other the business, and on one particular occasion, Duke was really giving Marty a hard time. Marty stood behind Duke, who was lighting a cigarette. He noticed Duke had a handkerchief hanging out of his back pocket. Marty took his lighter and lit the handkerchief on fire. As it started to burn, he said, "You know Duke, you think you're really hot ****. You really burn my ass." And just as he finished the sentence, Duke began jumping up and down to put the fire out. This was all taking place 44 floors up on red steel. Everyone was in hysterics watching such a scene. For me, it broke the tension of being so scared on the steel.

One day I was having lunch with Duke on the street. I saw someone I knew and waved to him, but I didn't seem to get his attention. Duke said, "Look kid, when you're a working man you are invisible to the suits." That was a valuable lesson. While these stories are just a taste of some of the antics these guys would pull, I did learn a lot from them.

Later on in my ironworking career, I was assigned to the AT&T building on 6th Avenue and 42nd Street. Today it stands as the MetLife building—the very same building where my office was so many years later.

Consider what you may have learned from early jobs or experiences. Keeping track of these early times may give you useful clues to situations throughout your life.

My experience as an iron worker not only taught me what it means to face one's fears, but it also provided me with a front row seat to a momentous incident. This incident would later help me put my finger on the source of trouble for a whole host of situations. I didn't know it at the time, but that summer job in college would teach me more in one day than some of my classes could in a semester. One day I was up on the beams at the 44th floor. Supported by multiple one-inch cables in tent configuration was a derrick, which lifted the steel up from the street. When you're in denial you get used to watching these heavy loads travel up and down like pick-up-sticks in a kid's fist. At some point you let yourself forget that there are laws of nature at play. No matter how strong the cable or how skilled the crane operator, you should never lose respect for basic physics. We would walk right under those loads, forgetting that safety codes warned us to walk around.

There was a rumor that we were beginning to lift heavier loads because the bosses wanted to get the job done faster. One day I had my back to the crane and I heard a big "clang!" When I turned around, a cable had cut loose from the rig and was now swishing across the deck I was standing on—on a 24-inch beam. I had to avoid it. If it hit me, it would cut me in half. At that moment, everyone there was concerned. Would the crane hold up? Would the engineer be able to lower the steel, which was now halfway up the building? The crane groaned and began to shake. What would happen if the other cables snapped? We were in Midtown Manhattan, at the intersection of 42nd Street and 6th Avenue. We were there, transfixed. How many helpless people would be killed?

There was nothing we could do to stop the impending disaster. One by one the other cables began to snap, and the whole load of steel fell down into the street. By some miracle only one person was killed. I never lost the freshness of that horrific experience, or its lesson about the boundaries and limitations of human enterprise.

In college, I volunteered for Catholic Big Brothers of America when I wasn't working as a nightclub bouncer with my football buddies. At the time, the irony of a guy with no father serving as a father figure was lost on me. But the irony of getting home from work at 4 a.m. and then meeting a few hours later to be a role model did register. I did what I could, getting these kids to the pool, to the movies—just to have a good time. But I also learned at a young age what all fathers eventually learn: There comes a time when you are not the person a teenage boy wants sitting next to him at the movies.

I became a Big Brother on the recommendation of none other than Father Rushmore, the same Jesuit priest who reminded me years later to continue questioning. Volunteering some of my time to give boys a mentor in their lives didn't seem like a big deal back then. I hope I did some good for those kids. But like so many other things, Big Brothers started out as something I wanted to do for others and became a major catalyst in my own life.

I've been married for over 30 years to my wife, Geraldine. She has been through everything with me. She is my partner, in the best sense of the word. And if I hadn't volunteered for Big Brothers, I might never have met her. She was working for Catholic Charities when I was a Big Brother. We met, and the rest is history.

This alone would have made my participation in Big Brothers worthwhile. However, when the time came to choose a career path, it was my Big Brother connections that pointed me toward the life insurance business. There was a guy who used to play for the New York Giants who was also involved with Catholic Big Brothers. He was the one who told me, "This might be a good career for you." I could not have imagined where my decision would lead me to. I took his advice, partly because I looked up to him as an athlete, partly because of my admiration for his involvement with Big Brothers, and partly because it was a job and I needed one.

The company I joined on his recommendation, Home Life, had a college division that allowed you to sell to your peers. When I went in to talk with them, they were all over me to join, and it made me feel good. I was the only rep on campus for Home Life.

Soon after that, I was walking up the driveway of one of my first customers—a relative of mine—for what I thought would be a pretty straightforward conversation about the policy we'd discussed over the phone.

As I rang the doorbell, I was naively unprepared for what was to come. I'd plowed through linemen and defied gravity on a sliver of steel, but I did not expect the body blow my own family members would deliver upon me that day.

I could tell he was already worked up. I followed him as he marched into the study of his family's Westchester home. We faced each other over an antique desk that probably cost more than the family car we couldn't afford. I could not comprehend what he was rambling on about.

Moments later, his father strode into the room. He grabbed the documents out of my hand and flung them into my face. "How dare you peddle this garbage to my son!" he shouted. He disparaged me personally, questioning my motives and running down the company I worked for. It was a tremendous shock.

I never told my mother what happened, but for days I asked myself if this was the right line of work for me. I wasn't sure there was any job that was worth this kind of assault on my self-esteem, but I stayed with it. I'm sure I thought I knew why at the time. Today I know that the answer still lies deep in my subconscious.

My determination to stay with my job began with my mother. She was the only parent I ever knew, and I wanted to do the right thing by her. As the stories of my youth unfolded in my adult mind while watching that PSA, it became apparent that there was another specter I'd eventually have to acknowledge. One of the strongest influences in my life had the biggest impact through his absence. My absent father reverberated everywhere; he wasn't there, yet he shaped my entire life story.

My mother at work, my sisters at home postponing college, my own early introduction to work—all of it happened because he wasn't there. I was a father figure to young boys without fathers when I had no father of my own. My father wasn't there to tell me what to say to the young boys. On the football field, among the steel workers—my father was not there. And he was not there when another man's father hurled my paperwork and my dignity in my face. Although he couldn't help that, he could have left a very different legacy.

At that moment, two trains of thought converged. First, the questions bubbled in: What had motivated me? Why did I put myself in these positions? What had I missed in my mother's eyes on the day she moved in with us? And second, a slow burn started, the flames of which would not erupt for another five years.

Have you faced rejection from someone whose opinion mattered a great deal to you?

What effect has rejection had on your self-esteem? Your work habits?

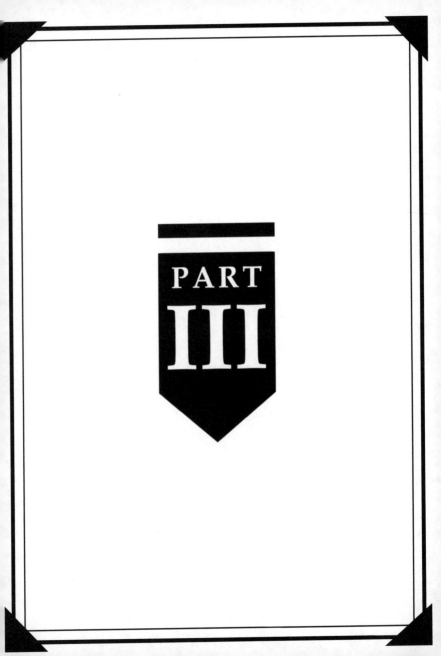

PART

III

CHAPTER 8
Coming to Terms

"A man is about as big as the things that make him angry."

— WINSTON CHURCHILL

Sometimes you'll hear people say, "Don't sweat the small stuff." I think Churchill was making the same point with his quote, but from a stronger perspective. When you are angry, you may think it is about something insignificant, when it's actually rooted in something deeper. If you search for the source of your anger, it is possible to find what really matters to you. I used to think that someone hanging up on me during a sales call frustrated me because it was rude. I later discovered that what really upset me was that the person hung up on a chance to do what's right for his family. My anger, it turned out, was about the basic injustice of families left without resources at their greatest time of need.

I had never made the connection between growing up without a father and my choice to go into insurance until I saw that PSA in 1999—more than 10 years after I had lost my mother and almost 50 years since I had lost my dad. I had viewed my life story as having played itself out due to circumstances. My career was more about my choices, my plans, and my drive for success.

I showed the PSA video at a fee-based financial planning meeting. I had used material before to tap into the emotions of the audience, but this was different. Not only was I tapping into the planners' emotions, but I, too, was experiencing an emotional connection. I became aware that my own story could unlock a deeper understanding of the good that financial planners do. At the time, we were all mourning the passing of a dear friend and MetLife colleague. We remembered how he had affected us and the lives of so many people he had served over the years. As we praised our friend for the way he changed lives for the better, I realized that emotion was not only a presentation approach; it had a place in inspiring sales reps to see how their products can help people.

I let the questions begin. It would be fruitful to look at my life experience from a new perspective. What did any of those things mean? Choices, plans, success. How much is in my control and how much "just happens"? How do I tell the difference between the two, and what difference does it make to the rest of the world? It turns out that I cared more than I realized. How my decisions affected others had everything to do with my choice of a career. I came to understand that my personal and professional lives were intertwined in ways I had never imagined. The seeds that had been planted along the way had begun to germinate: my mother's courage, my father's absence, my sports experiences, my career path, and the wisdom of experts in both professional and philosophical areas.

Throughout the '90s, I sought out the wisdom of experts from a wide range of disciplines. I read voraciously, and I thanked my mentor for giving me the permission I hadn't known I was seeking: to examine my life's journey.

From the time Father Rushmore encouraged me to continually question, I had peeled back the layers of my life in search for meaning. It was inevitable that the search would someday reach its core.

In the spring of 2004, I spoke before the MDRT gathering. I began to see the bits and pieces of my life story as something more cohesive. The stretch into my personal anthropology was reaching critical mass. No sooner had I started to work on my presentation than I tapped into a hidden vein of anger under the surface of my professional exterior. The anger I felt was a legitimate response to an ancient hurt. Even so, it surprised me. I knew I had to accept it and move on. But for the moment, it was a part of everything I did and said.

I'm including an excerpt from the end of the presentation here. As you read it, picture me with my fists clenched while I told my own story — and actually, heard my own story — for the first time. Imagine how it felt to speak to 8,600 people about the father I never knew. It will sound familiar to you now, since you've read the preceding pages, but here you will get a sense of the anger that overtook me as I shared it for the first time.

"When I was nine months old, my successful attorney father died without life insurance. My mother had to work as a secretary to raise all of us. My sisters did not go to college at the appropriate time, even though one got a full scholarship. The girls had to work to make sure the boys could get through school. Mother worked hard. I graduated and then Mother became ill. She began to see that she would be dependent. She said, 'I would be inconvenient.' She then willed herself to die. That is why she is not here to see her son on the main platform of the Million Dollar Round Table.

People do not deserve to go out like that. I want to know where was the person of significance, the advocate, who could have taken my father, pushed him up against a wall and said, 'Don't you understand you have to have life insurance? I'm advocating for your wife, because if you're gone, life could be miserable for her.' Where was the person who advocated for my sisters when they were denied a college education at the appropriate time? Where is the advocate, even now, for my father, whose youngest son stands in front of you now? The only legacy that my father left was leaving us alone.

You have to understand what your sacred trust is. You have to overcome your call reluctance. It has to come from the heart to go out and find people like my mother, because you have to protect them. You have to help people. Ask the question they cannot ask without you, which is what would happen if I were not here to take care of my family?

Finally, you have permission to be confrontational with people because you are dealing with their most precious assets—their children and their legacy. If someone is disrespectful to you and treats you like a used car salesman tell them this: What I do for a living is protecting the innocent when someone dies prematurely. I provide a worry-free retirement that people cannot outlive. I protect their assets when they become ill. I provide a legacy when they die because I live a life of significance."

This all came out spontaneously in that 2004 presentation to the MDRT. I had channeled a surge of pure rage; I was angry with my father for leaving his family unprotected.

There it was, the connective tissue between my personal journey and my chosen profession. Who could possibly be better suited to work on behalf of the beneficiaries of insurance clients—as I did for over three decades—than a person who knew firsthand what it meant when those insurance policies weren't in place? It had taken me all those years to fully appreciate how my father's untimely death and unwise decision had set the course for my mother's life. This included her ultimate need to be taken in by us at the end of her life, as well as the lives of my siblings and my own. How could I have been unaware of this burr in my saddle, prodding me to teach people to think about the ones who rely on them?

I have always known, in every fiber of my being, that nothing is more important than insuring the wellbeing of those who depend on you. This is the basis of our calling in the insurance business.

CHAPTER 9
Finding Julius

Art's Story

The story of **Art Steinberg** and his family shows how a reverse situation from my own has had such an impact for generations. Ira Horowitz was the life insurance agent who sold the policy in this story. Sixty years and three generations later, the family still remembers his name.

> On the night of my brother's bar mitzvah, family members flew in from all over to help us celebrate his passage to manhood. It was the summer of 1954. My father was a young man at 45 years old. He died that night. It was sudden and unexpected, and it transformed a joyous family gathering into an occasion for mourning.
>
> Like most women at the time, my mother did not work outside the home. She had two sons, aged nine and thirteen, a mortgage, and a lifetime of expenses ahead of her. However, my father had met an insurance agent just a few weeks earlier. He had purchased a sizeable life insurance policy. That policy paid a lump sum of $20,000, which more than

covered the mortgage, and a continuing monthly benefit of $263 per month.

I remember the exact amount because 10 years later, in my sophomore year of college, my mother died. But the checks kept coming through to my last month of school. I remember receiving the letter saying that the enclosed payment was the final one. Incredible. I thought how smart my father was to have come up with a plan like that – to put two sons through college, and to keep the family home decades after his death.

Though I didn't want to take anything away from my father for making such a good decision, I knew that he was not very educated in financial matters. I realized the credit was due in large part to the insurance agent who sat him down and said to him, "You know, Julius, if all of a sudden you're not here tomorrow, what is going to keep your family in their home and get your boys through college?" My father must have given him the basic numbers to work with, and the result was that it was all paid through to my graduation. The impact of this was enormous; it goes far beyond the financial aspects of our lives. Somehow everything is connected. Had my father not done that, my brother and I would not have received college educations. I wouldn't have met the woman I married, and we wouldn't have *had children together. So that decision did not affect one generation; it endures. Because of my father's choice, all my children have been educated, I have grandchildren, and they're the beneficiaries, too.*

Fifty-six years ago, that one agent had a conversation that transformed the lives of multiple generations and is still affecting lives to this day. As an insurance agent, I never lose sight of the potential we have in this business to change lives. My challenge to everyone in the insurance business, especially new agents, is this: We need to help more people like Julius. To protect those who care for their families, those who would never want to leave their closest relatives unprotected. To assist those who may not have the ability to make all the right financial decisions on their own. To show how life-changing the choice to purchase insurance can be.

I like to joke around about "Joe's Interesting and Amazing Facts." It's my proprietary research that illustrates this: Everybody dies. I don't like to dwell on this fact. It doesn't make sense to sit around and worry about it, but we have to accept it and prepare for it. Denying it won't change it. My father lost sight of this reality. Possibly the most upsetting part of the story is that he had a policy. There was a time when he grasped the importance of insurance, but he let it go. And the wheels were set in motion for five lives to change after one ended.

As the roots of my anger were exposed, I became furious about the lack of recognition for our industry's contribution to the lives of so many people. It was as though my awareness of my experience as an unprotected child gave me a newfound passion to speak on behalf of all who are vulnerable. It resonated in the core of my being. The recognition of my mother and my wife emboldened me on behalf of those who might benefit from long-term care protection.

For years, most insurance professionals have approached prospecting with all the relish of receiving a root canal. They all but apologize for engaging in a conversation that every responsible adult ought to have. Somewhere along the line, many in our profession bought into a skewed perspective about what we do. In the heat of my anger, I felt a flash of clarity. We shouldn't feel like beggars, we should feel like saints. As Csaba Sziklai said, we are "advocates who have little or no voice in the decision to buy insurance despite the fact that [clients'] lives can be seriously affected by [the] presence or absence thereof." I watched the reaction to my 2004 presentation, feeling just as surprised and moved by my passion as everyone else in the room.

The Steinberg family's story lives on in their son Justin, underscoring the value of facing painful moments with courage. While I truly appreciated Art Steinberg's first story, he seemed somewhat distracted when we were taping him. Later on I discovered that his son, Justin, had recently died. This is Justin's story.

Justin's Story

A scholarship represents an individual or a group who wants another person to have the opportunity to pursue their dreams. You may have walked by a plaque or read a graduation program and wondered about an unfamiliar name. This is the story behind one of those names. In the words of his father, Art Steinberg, Justin was "just the greatest son. I can't remember him ever giving us a bad time. And his personality — he just had the best sense of humor. He was fun to be around."

Justin was never able to graduate from college. Just before finals, only six weeks before the end of his sophomore year, he fell into the final relapse of a long, debilitating and ultimately fatal illness. Throughout his ordeal, Justin always thought of others first. He worried that he might trouble the nurses. He was concerned about his parents. But they reassured him, and it truly gave him comfort to know that the financial hardship of his illness was alleviated by a policy his parents bought for him when he was a child — one with a disability waiver that paid premium while he was ill, guaranteeing his legacy to others.

As Justin's parents faced the inevitable loss of their son, his mother made a "nonnegotiable, irreversible decision" to honor her son's memory in a way that reflected his selfless and giving nature. Knowing how much Justin loved learning, and more specifically Mary Washington College (now University of Mary Washington), his mother established the Justin Steinberg Scholarship there. Funded by the proceeds of his life insurance policy and nurtured for posterity by continued investment, the scholarship fund in Justin's name provides a need-based award. It enables one student each year to attend the historic, private university just a few hours south of our nation's capital and gain an excellent higher education that they otherwise could not have achieved.

The first recipient, Fiona Cobb, was one of 10 children in a Navy family. She wrote the Steinbergs a beautiful letter of appreciation. They knew they had made the right decision.

Let me tell you about the Cobbs. They have four biological children and three adopted children. Foster care came to them one day and asked if the Cobbs could take care of three kids for about two weeks. Two weeks turned into two years, and the Cobbs wound up adopting the children. Who could think of a recipient more deserving of this scholarship than a member of the Cobb family — a family that did so much good for others?

Justin's name will live on for generations. "Long after we're gone, students will still receive the Justin Steinberg scholarship," his mother proudly stated. More than his name, Justin's generous spirit lives on. It has branched out into the lives of students and their families, their accomplishments and contributions to society. "That is the miracle of life insurance," Justin's father said plainly. "The scholarship is really a way for Justin to live on because it is exactly the way he was. He cared about people."

THE IRA HOROWITZ LEGACY PRESENTED

In 2009, I was on the main platform at the GAMA LAMP conference, an organization of 3,500 insurance managers from around the world. In my presentation, I told the story of the Ira Horowitz legacy and of all the people who were impacted by that sale in 1954. I described Julius Steinberg, who bought the original policy from Ira Horowitz. Upon his death, his son Art Steinberg was the beneficiary. Art attributes much of his success to the policy his father provided. Then, after his son Justin unfortunately passed, a scholarship was founded in Justin's name at his alma mater. The first recipient was Fiona Cobb.

Unbeknownst to the audience, I had the Steinbergs and the Cobbs at the presentation. I had them come on stage with me. They received a standing ovation. Everyone in the audience was able to see four generations that have benefitted from a single sale made in 1954.

To my knowledge, no one before has traced a sale this far back in time. It is one thing to say that you can benefit generations of people as a financial services expert, but it's another to see the people who have been affected in the flesh. This illustrates our need to spend more time thinking about the impact we have on others.

In 2012, I was giving a speech that focused on the Ira Horowitz legacy. At the end of the speech, I was approached by **David and Kathy McBride**. Both were in tears. David told me his daughter, Adrianna, had been killed in a car accident. When he saw the legacy unfold in my presentation, he was inspired to keep the memory of his daughter alive. He established two scholarships in the name of Adrianna: one for the English department and the other need-based.

After setting up the scholarships, Kathy and David expressed their feelings on the outcome. "As Joe related the power of that story and the miracle of what life insurance can do, it had such an impact on us," said David. Kathy added, "This was an incredibly healing experience for us to bring a lifetime of change to a student. All of the students that earned scholarships were the first in their families to attend college. Every one of them has sent us thank you notes that say they wouldn't be able to do without this, and that they'll make Adrianna proud."

I learned that as of 2013, more than 10 students have had their college tuition paid for between the Steinbergs and the McBrides. Ira Horowitz's legacy spans more than four generations, and every person affected by him knows his name.

The key question is: Did Ira Horowitz recognize this? Odds are, he was happy for the sale. Maybe he validated his contract or was able to go to the leaders' conference somewhere. Imagine how he would feel about himself knowing he had done so much for so many? His self-esteem would double if he knew what a positive impact he has had on all those people, not to mention the fact that they all know exactly who he was. Ira Horowitz provided an intergenerational gift for many families to come. For everyone in the financial services industry, Ira Horowitz's gift is to show you your impact. By focusing on your impact, you know that people who are not even born yet will remember you long after you are gone. For everyone in the financial services industry, this is the true compensation for our work.

The financial services culture needs to put more emphasis on these stories. We must build a culture of pride and high self-esteem centered on client and societal impact. A culture such as this would inspire financial services reps to overcome the negativity and rejection they face. If you are in the business, how many lives have you impacted? And if you are considering joining financial services, tell me another profession that can have such a remarkable impact. In life, it's not what you get—it's what you become. Ira Horowitz and all of you in financial services are heroes.

Why would you be in this business and miss such an impact?

Harmony in Nature: Chief Seattle's Speech

In our Western culture, with our emphasis on individualism, we focus on our separateness from other people and from nature. In Native American traditions, the interconnectedness of all living things is said to bring harmony to one's life. This belief sustained the Native American people through many trials. In time, I would come to value the words of the Native American leader, **Chief Seattle**, as the quintessential manifestation of coming to terms with a painful experience. Chief Seattle, for whom the city of Seattle, Washington, is named, was a brave and eloquent leader of the Suquamish and Duwamish tribes which controlled much of the area around the northern Puget Sound in the 1800s. He was greatly respected by his people, and his prophetic vision of a world without respect for nature has earned him respect far beyond the cultural boundaries of his time. His legendary speech delivered in 1854 has inspired historians and environmentalists for more than a century. I've included the modern interpretation of the speech by Ted Perry here:

We just got word from your president back in Washington that he wants to buy our land. But how can you buy and sell the sky? The land? The idea is strange to us. All parts of this earth are sacred to my people. Every shining pine needle, every sandy shore. Every meadow is all holy in the memory and experience of my people. We are part of the earth and

Every meadow is all holy in the memory and experience of my people. We are part of the earth and it is part of us. The perfumed flowers. These are our sisters. The bear, the deer, the eagle, these are our brothers. Each ghostly reflection in the clear waters of the lake tells of the events with the voice of my grandfather's father. The rivers, these are our brothers. They carry our canoes and feed our children. If you buy our land, know that the air is precious to us. Know that the air shares its spirit with all the life it supports. The wind that gave my great-grandfather his first breath also received his last sigh. This we know.

The earth does not belong to man. Man belongs to the earth. All things are connected like the blood that binds us together. Man did not create the web of life, he simply is a strand in it. What he does to the web, he does to himself. Your destiny is a mystery to us. What will happen when all the buffalo are slaughtered? What will happen when all the secret corners of the forest are heavy with the scent of many men? And the view of the ripe hills is blotted by talking wires? It's the end of living, and the beginning of survival. When the last Red Man and his wilderness is gone, and his memory is that of a cloud going over the prairie, will there be any memory of my people left? We love this land like the newborn loves its mother's heartbeat.

So if you buy this land, love it as we have loved it. Care for it as we have cared for it. Hold in your mind

> *the memories of the land when you receive it, and*
> *preserve it for all children. Love the land the way God*
> *loves you, because this we know, no man be he Red*
> *Man or White Man can stand alone. Because we're*
> *brothers after all.*[9]

This speech was delivered at a time when Chief Seattle and his people were about to lose everything, yet his philosophy of balance with nature caused him to pity the civilization that was taking the land. You see, in the Western tradition, we view nature as something to be conquered. That's why we cut down the forest and kill buffalo, disregard gravity by lifting heavy loads of steel, and defy all reason by offering subprime mortgages to people for whom the financial burden would become too great to bear. In a culture without harmony, you can be enriched, but never fulfilled.

Chief Seattle gives the best definition of what the Million Dollar Round Table calls "the complete person": knowledge of where you came from, stewardship while you are here, and legacy when you die. Notice how he gives human attributes to parts of nature. To him, the whole planet was alive. Also notice his reference to the web of life. Look at the role Ira Horowitz played in the web of life. Insuring Julius Steinberg allowed for his proceeds to ensure his son Art a good life. Ira's legacy continued as Art insured his son, Justin, who fell ill and sadly passed away.

[9] Written by Ted Perry, inspired by a speech attributed to Chief Seattle.

The proceeds of Justin's policy assure the college tuition for many more to come.

In the Service of Others

As part of the Living a Life of Significance™ program, we asked agents to tell us the stories they considered pivotal in their careers. A story submitted by **Bob Weaver**, a 60-year-old veteran of the business, makes a powerful case to boost self-esteem in our industry. Here is his story.

> *Back in 1945, two young Air Force pilots were hitchhiking back to base after being on leave. It was the dead of winter in central Massachusetts, and the snow had drifted well over their heads on the side of the road. The two had just completed rigorous training and both qualified for a prestigious unit. They were ready for deployment. A Good Samaritan pulled over and let them into his car. The kindly driver told the pair that he would need to make a few stops along the way, but he would be glad to take the young men to Springfield if they would have the patience for his schedule.*
>
> *After the second stop, the driver explained that he was collecting life insurance premiums from his clients (they were just a few dollars back then). He preferred to do it in person so he could stay in touch with every individual he served. Before thinking*

much about it, one of the soldiers responded as he might have to one of the guys in the barracks — without much respect, but intending no real harm.

"That's quite a racket you've got there," he quipped.

The driver's face changed abruptly, and he steered the car off the road. He was so close to the snow bank that the passenger door could not have been opened.

"You can climb out over me, or you can stay here and listen," he said sternly. "At the next stop I'm going to make, I won't be collecting a payment — I'll be delivering one. Even though it won't bring back the father and husband of that household, it will be more money than they've probably ever seen in one check. And it will make all the difference in the lives of that family. So make no mistake, what I do is no racket. I am serving my clients in a way that can keep them going when they need it most. You boys should understand the importance of service. Am I right?"

They did understand. And one of those Air Force pilots went on to be an extremely successful producer, who considered this story the one that changed his life. He said it motivated him to find a career that gave his life significance. That young pilot was Bob Weaver.

In the story, I hear the same passion in the words of the agent serving each and every one of his clients in person. This man inspired another to devote 60 years to following those footsteps.

A life of significance is not a sprint; it's a marathon. The challenge of living a significant life is that there is not much instant gratification. Significant people must focus on what's important, not just what is popular. This can be difficult at times. One of the quotes that has helped me deal with this reality came from the philosopher **Reinhold Niebuhr**. He wrote:

> *"Nothing that is worth doing can be achieved in our lifetime; therefore we must be saved by hope. Nothing which is true or beautiful or good makes complete sense in any immediate context of history; therefore we must be saved by faith. Nothing we do, however virtuous, can be accomplished alone; therefore we must be saved by love. No virtuous act is quite as virtuous from the standpoint of our friend or foe as it is from our standpoint. Therefore we must be saved by the final form of love which is forgiveness."*

A NEW GLOBAL FORCE IN THE WORLD

There is another powerful global force entering our lives, and that is the new Pope. It is remarkable that he is both the first Pope from the Americas and also the first Jesuit Pope. But it is most remarkable because his name is Francis I, named after Francis of Assisi—a Franciscan. This is the order that focuses on the care and stewardship of the poor. He will be a powerful voice to speak about our obligations to others.

I recently listened to *The Power of Intention* by **Dr. Wayne Dyer**. In it, his daughter sang the prayer attributed to St. Francis.

> *Lord, make me an instrument of your peace,*
> *Where there is hatred, let me sow love;*
> *Where there is injury, pardon;*
> *Where there is doubt, faith;*
> *Where there is despair, hope;*
> *Where there is darkness, light;*
> *Where there is sadness, joy.*

Don't think of this prayer as Catholic. Don't think of it as Christian. Don't even think of it as religious. Think of it as a meditation to change the way you see things, because as Wayne Dyer says, "When you change the way you see things, the things you see change."

CHAPTER 10

Digging Deeper

The best way to deal with anything painful is to face it head on, as Chief Seattle did. No sooner had I made this realization than my mind filled with images of my days on the football field. Now, the insurance business has no shortage of sports-related stories and metaphors. I knew that part of my story would fit neatly into one of these formulaic tales. There is no doubt that my head-down determination to take out the guy in front of me, no matter what his size, had been translated into a similar drive in situations such as getting back to New York from that disastrous PaineWebber Club Med trip I mentioned earlier.

But there was more to my memories about college sports than clichés about motivation. When I played football at Fordham, I played in the exact position that was once filled by the legendary Vince Lombardi. Lombardi died of cancer the year I started college. Before then, he had been a winning coach for the Green Bay Packers. When he died, the Super Bowl trophy was renamed in his honor.

When I was playing in his spot, I liked to joke that Lombardi almost came to life for me. You can imagine the influence this icon had on young men my age, men who grew up watching and playing football. So to stand on the field in his position gave me a great sense of responsibility and connection to the Hall of Famer. The tougher the situation, the louder I could hear Lombardi in my ear and feel him over my shoulder. When I made All East, I gave a nod of gratitude to my "patron saint of offense," Vince Lombardi.

But, perhaps the most meaningful lesson I learned from playing college sports came from the fact that I had experience on both the football and the rugby team. Traditional American football, while a team sport, predominantly emphasizes the starting team. Vince Lombardi would say, "I don't play my eleven best, I play my best eleven." This inspires teamwork. The difference is that in football, only the first team plays. Many college and high school football players hardly ever see time on the field. Furthermore, there is no way you meet the other team if you're not on the starting team. And you would never see them after the game. The culture of American football is such that meeting others is incidental to playing the game.

In rugby, everybody plays. If you're not on the "A" team, you are on the "B" or "C" team. It is customary after the game to party with the other team. You meet and forge relationships with people who have common interests. So in the rugby culture, being on the team no matter what string you are is incidental to meeting and socializing with others.

The most memorable opponent I faced throughout my college career was number 57 from Georgetown. Because we both started as freshmen, we lined up against each other once a year for four years. He was distinctive because he had no teeth in his mouth except his two canines. It was like lining up against Count Dracula; we would absolutely kill each other. Every time we lined up, it reminded me of the Ali versus Frazier fight.

At the end of the game, we would seek each other out and say, "See you next year." After we both graduated, we lost touch. In 1976, my rugby team, The New York Athletic Club, was playing the Harvard Business School. At the end of a game, I put on a Fordham football windbreaker. My opposite number looked at the emblem and asked me if I played at Fordham. I replied yes. He pulled his teeth out—it was Number 57! What a great reunion.

There's an important point to make about the player experience between football and rugby. The cultures are different; one emphasizes the game while the other emphasizes relationships.

Having played both, it is my opinion that American football is more violent. The equipment is not protection—it is a weapon. Football is a game of *collision*, predicated on the taking and defending of territory. As a result, there are more frequent all-out collisions. The play ends, the teams regroup, catch their breath, and do it all over again. Rugby is a game of possession. The key is to keep possession of the ball—to keep passing it or to set it up for the forwards to keep possession of the ball. The ebb and flow of yardage is less important. As a result you don't always get the *consistent* big hits. Just look at all the revelations about concussions in American football.

It's a function of culture. Before, I said that I was probably hired at MetLife based on my knowledge and experience with annuities in the investment world. But I have been influenced as much by culture and human behavior as I have been by product. When I first arrived at MetLife after years in the fast-moving Wall Street environment, the pace seemed glacial to me. Remembering the importance of connecting with people to foster a common understanding, I wanted to set up conference calls with agents around the country. In 1990, MetLife—like many big companies—didn't have the kind of phones you need for these calls. My response was to send someone out to RadioShack to buy one. It seemed like a simple thing, but it was revolutionary at the time. With a $200 conference phone, we broke through layers of hierarchy and years of separatist behaviors. Agents, actuaries, and investment department reps were now all on the phone together talking about what they actually do, rather than wondering who is keeping them from what they want to do. Before these calls, which quickly became standard practice, everyone had communicated by letter. Now people were able to value each other's contributions, exchange ideas, and get things done more effectively.

What barriers have you faced that you might break down with a bit of creativity?

We sometimes fail to appreciate how rapidly our culture has changed in the past 20 years. Some of those changes came with advances in technology; some came through other forces. For example, the huge influx of women in the workforce has changed business culture in ways I wish my mother could have experienced. I remember all too well how casually my male colleagues would toss out a phrase like, "Let's bring the girls in to take notes." The person who came in would not be a "girl" at all, but a woman who clearly deserved the respect of being treated as a peer. I would always think of my mother, single-handedly raising her four children and going in to work for men who referred to her as a "girl." It's important to remember advances such as these, so we can keep them intact. Respect is a critical element in a healthy culture. For both coworkers and customers, respect is just plain good for business.

This brings us to our current situation in the early 21st century. Now, more than ever, the products offered by insurance companies are of tremendous value to the consumer. People no longer have the kind of security that old-style, defined benefit plans offered. The sheer volume of financial choices can be overwhelming for the average person trying to make sound decisions. Beyond that, the lessons of history continue to demonstrate that if people can tolerate volatility (the price one pays for greater long-term total return of equities), they will do better. The problem is getting people to deal with the emotional extremes of euphoria at the top and panic at the bottom.

Clients need a partner. They need someone or an entity that can talk with them and take some of the fear away. The real risk people face is not the risk to principal, but the risk to purchasing power. For a 65-year-old nonsmoking couple with a life expectancy of 30 years, $100,000 at age 65 needs to be $230,000 in 30 years at 3% inflation. That requires them to have some form of an equity position. But how can you help people stay in equities and handle volatility, which time and time again people fail to do?

For the insurance industry, the crisis that began in 2007 introduced the perfect opportunity to reassert the value of protection and income products in the face of financial insecurity. To be sure, the crisis was triggered by the same sort of unsafe practices that always lead to financial crises. In Reinhart and Rogoff's book, *This Time is Different*,[10] no less than eight centuries of "financial folly" are documented, which leads to the conclusion that we will see more bubble-and-burst scenarios for as long as human beings are dealing with financial matters.

In the past, economists have almost universally dismissed emotion as a secondary decision-making factor. Experts in many fields — science, sociology, and, yes, even economics — are consistently telling us that few important decisions are made without emotion. The protection of one's family in the case of death or disability and the protection against the financial burden imposed by long-term care costs are undeniably emotional issues. It would be virtually impossible to have an objective conversation about topics like these, in which the issues truly register with the person whose family's wellbeing is at stake. My own childhood and my mother's last years are the quintessential stories of

[10] Carmen M. Reinhart and Kenneth S. Rogoff, *This Time is Different: Eight Centuries of Financial Folly* (Princeton, NJ: Princeton University Press, March 3, 2011).

how a fateful decision to forego the security of insurance coverage can shape a lifetime. As insurance professionals, part of our responsibility is to make sure people connect their decisions with the faces of those who will be affected by them. Charts, tables, and graphs should come into play only after the personal and emotional connection is made.

Once I recognized the connection between my personal and professional paths, I started to see links everywhere: the connection between Catholic Big Brothers and my first job at Home Life; my determination on the football field and my bold step into the department head position at PaineWebber; my respect for my mother and my rejection of sexist comments; my dedication to life protection products and my anger toward my father.

When the financial disaster struck in 2008, the financial firms began teetering like giant dominoes threatening to flatten the entire economy. I began to make the association that has served me best. This time my view was from the 40th floor of 1095 Avenue of the Americas — a floor I once walked on when it was open steel beams. From that building, in 1971, I heard the horrific snap of cables succumbing to forces of the heavy steel loads.

At the same building in 2008, this time safely behind walls and windows, someone rushed into our meeting and informed us that AIG would be declaring bankruptcy in 30 minutes. The last company that I would have expected to have trouble was AIG. It had a great track record for profits and earnings. They always seemed to be doing the right thing. Standing in the very building that I helped build, I instantly thought of the load too heavy. However, this time it wasn't steel; it was subprime mortgages. Rather than defying gravity, some very smart people decided to defy common sense. They thought they could give mortgages to people they weren't sure had the ability to pay them back. The premise was that real estate prices would continue to rise. Since they could securitize the mortgages, they sold them to other institutions that should have known better because they wanted a higher yield.

It worked for a while, but eventually the load became too heavy. The first cable to snap was Countrywide, then Bear Stearns, Lehman Brothers, Merrill Lynch, and finally AIG. Every last one of those employees was betrayed by the decision of senior management to defy common sense and act irresponsibly for short-term gain.

In the West, we see nature as something to be conquered. That's why, as Chief Seattle said, we kill the buffalo. Or as we say in construction, we lift the heavy load. Conversely, in the East, the predominant thought is to be in harmony with nature. There, balance is necessary.

The lesson of the derrick is simple; it reaffirms one of my basic principles. I call it the Fairness Doctrine. There are three parties to the trade: a client, an intermediary, and a company. All three have to be a little sad.

If the client is ecstatic, you are giving it away. If the intermediary is ecstatic, you're paying too much. If the company is ecstatic, you couldn't sell it if your life depended on it. Balance among the three competing parties involved is the art of successful product development.

In that moment I saw in the clearest terms that there is nothing new under the sun. Just as rogue insurance companies such as Executive Life and Baldwin-United were invested in junk bonds and affiliated assets, so too were the wild revenue projections of the internet venture capital market. The subprime real estate market was not in the business of selling homes for people to live in. Instead, they acted as though houses were game pieces on a Monopoly board, placeholders. Ultimately, they all came crashing down.

Financial experts can tell you these things. You can read charts, graphs, and tables that demonstrate trends and confirm projection. But I would argue there is nothing more valuable than making that intuitive connection between the information you are digesting and your own personal, real-life experiences.

I have addressed how Bob Benmosche saved AIG. He recognized the value of the company and more importantly, the value of its employees. Jay Fishman, the chairman of Travelers, said that while Bob made shrewd business decisions, it was his ability to inspire human capital that was his greatest asset. He resisted efforts to break the company apart to avoid having thousands of employees lose their jobs and to keep clients from having to worry about their retirement savings or coverage.

Bob Benmosche knows that AIG needs to make money in the long run. He also understands that AIG exists to protect clients and their property. When a company understands its purpose, you will find that its decisions are not driven by short-term, quarterly results. Bob Benmosche brought back harmony and balance to AIG.

For my part, I felt fortunate that I had pursued my fascination with philosophy, spirituality, and other thought-provoking topics. I had not realized that these endeavors might become useful for insurance and business professionals beyond the ability to share relevant quotes in the course of my speaking engagements. I originally thought that my passion for learning was an exercise in personal growth. Now, the concepts, ideas, and expressions I had become familiar with found a new meaning within the right side of my brain, as left-brain dialogue moved into mainstream scientific and psychological circles.

When I wrote the first version of this book, the Gulf of Mexico had just suffered a devastating ecological and economic impact from a damaged deep-water well. The full effects will not be known for years to come. I cannot help but recall the sage commentary attributed to Chief Seattle on the dangers of environmental abuses. "Whatever befalls the earth, befalls the sons of the earth." Whether it is a man-made disaster that affects the ecology of the planet, or a man-made financial crisis that threatens the well-being of a nation, our actions never occur in a vacuum. When the culture of an industry--or worse, a society--fails to recognize our basic interconnection, the residual damage affects all.

It is essential to not only respect the laws of integrity and nature, but to take it a step further by helping restore harmony. One person's—or one company's—actions may not prevent bad things from happening, but they can add to the good side of the equation that keeps things in balance.

PART
IV

CHAPTER 11

Tapping the Well Within

"Be patient toward all that is unsolved in your heart and try to love the questions themselves, like locked rooms and like books that are now written in a very foreign tongue. Do not now seek the answers, which cannot be given to you because you would not be able to live them. And the point is, to live everything. Live the questions now. Perhaps you will then gradually, without noticing it, live along some distant day into the answer."

— RAINER MARIA RILKE, *LETTERS TO A YOUNG POET*

"We shall not cease from exploration, and the end of all our exploring will be to arrive where we started and know the place for the first time."

— T.S. ELIOT

I was fortunate to have Father Rushmore during college to give me permission to question, and later in life to remind me of the benefit of continually questioning. If you don't already have someone in your life that does the same for you, I hope that this book can serve this purpose.

The quotes in the beginning of this chapter remind us that we "live the questions." Answers come much later in life, if ever. To be hasty for answers is to miss out on precious life experiences. However, to rush around so often that you forget to question is perhaps the greatest loss.

I encourage you to be patient with those questions that surface every day. They are like an internal spring, filling a well of wisdom from which you can extract insights throughout your life and career. In this chapter, I will use the milestones that have set my personal journey in order to turn the spotlight on your voyage. My hope is that you recognize their universal qualities as they apply to you. This book is not supposed to help you learn more about Joe Jordan—it's intended to help you learn more about yourself.

The Vietnamese Buddhist monk Thich Nhat Hanh advises those who are angry to embrace their anger rather than push it away. This Eastern wisdom is sometimes difficult for a Western mind to grasp. We Westerners typically categorize emotions into the good and the bad. This may cost us opportunities to listen to parts of ourselves that can teach us important lessons.

Once my anger about my father welled to the surface, I had few options but to confront it. In doing so, I discovered it had much to tell me. My internal conflict brought a new perspective to my understanding of a few seminal moments in my life. In speaking with other insurance professionals, I have heard plenty of frustrations over the years. If we are honest with ourselves, we know that we must put ourselves in the line of fire, and we sometimes wonder why. Why do we take the risk of hearing NO hundreds of times in the course of our careers? Take a few minutes to go back and review some of the answers I've uncovered, and then try to translate them to your own experience. By answering the questions near the end of each section, you'll begin to see the emerging outline of your life of significance.

CHAPTER 12

A Mother's Struggle and a Son's Vocation

One common thread throughout my life has been a resolve that comes to my aid in critical moments. I find that this determination is fueled by my mother's strong example and my deep-seated unwillingness to let circumstances stop me. In this way, I was able to mentor fatherless boys though fatherless myself; to step into the shoes of the great Vince Lombardi; to climb stories high on the frame of a skyscraper, despite a serious fear of heights; and to pick up my broken ego from the floor of my cousin's study and go on to a successful 40+ year career in insurance. In a way, both my parents gave me a piece of what I needed to maintain such unswerving determination. My father planted a seed of anger in me that ultimately drove some positive results. But in the end, it was my mother's stoic grit that influenced my predisposition, instinctively kicking in at critical decision points and steering me toward my better self.

Determination may come naturally or it may require a conscious, concerted effort. In my experience, I have seen both. Make no mistake, it takes determination to work in this business. It comes most easily when you are convinced that what you've resolved to do is the right thing.

Who and what gave you some of your earliest inspiration?

How have you dealt with anger or unwanted emotions in your life?

What sources of strength do you draw from in your own history?

CHAPTER 13

The Crane and the Crash

In my personal story, determination led me through many situations, and often with tangential benefits that I couldn't have anticipated. For example, my determination to earn the money I needed for college put me where I needed to be to observe one of the most profound events of my life. The echo of that terrible construction accident in 1971 never left my ears or my psyche. As I think back to it now, I believe it taught me an invaluable lesson. As a metaphor for what happens when limits are breached, the snap of the cables, and all that led up to it, has become an internal barometer for me. It allows me to anticipate dangerous trends in markets, in relationships, and in life. I may not be able to prevent certain events from happening, but I can avoid walking under the hazardous load and help others to do the same.

I have talked about the nauseating sound that rang in my ears when the crane gave way. I heard it again in the spring of 2008 during the subprime debacle. In the 40 years that my career has spanned, there have been sufficient examples to illustrate that there are consequences for abandoning common sense and taking excessive risk.

Is there a personal experience or an observation from your professional life that serves as your internal barometer and has taught you any of the following?

1. To respect the laws of nature, including the natural tendencies of economics

2. To understand how things are designed, how they are intended to behave, or how to steer clear if they are being used in some other way

3. To stay alert to the environment and to assess situations for yourself

CHAPTER 14

Seeing Ghosts

That public service announcement about the elderly woman awakened a sense of awareness in me that I wish I'd had when my mother was still alive. In the days when her hospital bed was set up in our living room and my siblings were helping us take care of her, I know my mother felt loved. She knew we cared. But I will never know if she felt she had sacrificed her dignity after she couldn't maintain her independence any longer. I will never know if she felt that she was a burden to us. But she was still the duchess, and she would never have let on such an idea. I still wonder if I perhaps missed a look in her eyes, a look that gave her true feelings away.

From the moment I saw my mother's "ghost," I knew that I had to let people know how important it is to consider those feelings of dignity and independence when we speak to clients about long-term care insurance. These are not easy conversations to have among family members, especially if they happen after a need arises. These are the conversations that an insurance professional can feel so great about having.

Like the moment when you see the hidden picture in a Rorschach test, I can never "un-see" what I perceived in the PSA. It transformed the way I view long-term care insurance. I encourage you to reflect on what it might feel like to be left without options when care is necessary. This is particularly important because it is the rare individual who can ever hope to save enough to afford years of day-to-day care. Rather than living comfortably, as most likely would while living independently, many find themselves trying to unload assets to qualify for state or federal aid.

We must accept that some of the significance of life will not come to us in the moment it occurs, but later on, as we consider it from a distance.

Think back to some of the significant people in your life (grandparents, parents, spouses) when they faced a life-changing situation – or think ahead to how they would face a situation in the future.

Try to view each situation from the perspective of those who may not have a voice in their situation. List some of the emotions or considerations they may have.

Think about the human benefits our products deliver beyond the financial benefit: dignity, independence, and peace of mind. Imagine the impact those individuals would feel from experiencing those benefits.

CHAPTER 15

Thinking Beyond Yourself

"I think the person who takes a job in order to live—that is to say, for the money—has turned himself into a slave."

— JOSEPH CAMPBELL

It is difficult to sit down face-to-face with another person and convince him or her to do something if all you have in mind is your own personal gain. I spoke on the importance of thinking beyond yourself when you consider what motivates you. This applies to many situations and related products, whether they use a financial planning model or simply establish relationships with clients and help them choose what they need piecemeal. You will benefit the most by acknowledging how much your work can do for other people.

Bear the full weight of your emotional intelligence as you reassess your motivating factors. Considering others isn't a function of calculations or clinical data. Truly considering others means considering how their lives, or the lives of those they care about, can be sustained and improved through the peace of mind you bring to them.

Cast your net wide. There are very few people who are in such a safe financial position that you couldn't add some benefit to their lives. Think of the people you know personally, those you know tangentially, and those you may not know but who live and work in your community. See these people through new eyes.

Most people don't have someone watching out for their best interest. The pensions and other ironclad benefit plans that their grandparents benefited from are not available to them anymore. Today, you have the opportunity to help them restore some security and peace of mind. You can do this when you rely on your expertise and put their needs first. When you are coming from a stance of fairness and with a goal of being the advocate for the families and business partners of your clients, you can bring a positive, confident attitude to your conversations.

CHAPTER 16

So, Get Inspired

"We have a right to our labor, but not to the fruits of our labor."
— KRISHNA

One way to think beyond yourself is to get inspired! A lot of people mistake me for a motivational speaker, but how could *I* possibly motivate *you*? Look at the profession you've chosen. You talk to people about things they don't want to talk about. People don't want to come in and see you, and then when they *do* see you, they do not want to buy what you are selling. That takes plenty of motivation.

The problem with motivation, however, is that you have to drive it. I would offer that sometimes this business subjects you to so much negativity and rejection that motivation alone is not enough to sustain you. What you need to do is get inspired. The beauty of inspiration is that *it* drives *you*.

Inspiration is made up of two components: The first is your purpose, and the second is making a commitment to your purpose. What is your purpose? You have to recognize that you do something very significant. You could be the most important person in someone's life. A family continues, a business is sustained, or a legacy is spawned for generations by your activities. You must believe it and feel it.

This was driven home to me when I was privileged enough to share the stage with former Secretary of State and Chairman of the Joint Chiefs of Staff, General **Colin Powell.** He spoke the second day at the African American Insurance Conference, sponsored by the American College. He got up to the podium and said, "Some people like to have a mission. But I prefer *purpose!*"

Colin Powell expanded on the power of purpose in his book. "Mission goals and vision are conventional terms to indicate what organizations and individuals set out to accomplish. These are excellent and useful words, but I have come to prefer another and I believe better term: PURPOSE. Purpose is the destination of a vision. It energizes that vision, giving it force and drive." His fervent speech and book helped shape my own perspective on the meaning of purpose in the financial services industry.

Your unique purpose is to make certain that the money outlives the people. If you buy into this definition of your purpose, you must use protection products in your practice. People have to insure against what can go wrong to gain the luxury to invest in what can go right. The reality of this world is that people outlive their money, people get sick, and people die too soon.

Next is your value proposition. The advice you provide and the products you sell are worth far more than what your clients pay for them. Price is only an issue in the absence of value, so let's explore your value. You provide peace of mind when people die prematurely. You provide people with a worry-free retirement with an income they can't outlive so they can maintain their independence. You can protect that income if they get sick so that they maintain their dignity. And finally, you provide a legacy when they die.

Tell me if that is living a significant life. It's not enough to know this; you have to believe it. If you do, others will follow. Your beliefs drive your behavior. I am sure you have lofty goals that you desire to achieve. But if your goals are not in sync with your beliefs, your behavior will ultimately always manifest your beliefs.

If you are not convinced that you live a significant life, a life of service to others, then you are vulnerable to something no one in this business talks about: low self-esteem. Carter Woodson said that if you can determine how a man thinks, you don't have to worry about what he will do. If someone has an opinion of inferiority, you don't have to compel him to take an inferior position, because he'll get there all by himself. If you can make a person feel like an outcast, you don't have to tell him to leave—he will get up on his own.

How you feel about yourself is very important, because all chronic production issues are behavioral. A way to combat negative self-image is to create a cultural environment that celebrates the good you do. It is my belief that you will be inspired by contemplating the positive impact you have on others. It is this inspiration on top of your motivation that will sustain you through the negativity, rejection, and periodic bouts of low self-esteem.

So, how do you become inspired? Create a personal culture and insist that your agency craft an organizational culture that celebrates the positive impact you have on others. Do whatever it takes to create a culture that reminds you of the good you do, because culture manages when management is not there. You'll need a positive culture to deal with the changes that are coming. Believe in change, but never change what you believe.

Jack Keane, retired four-star general and former Vice Chief of Staff of the U.S. Army, is a major military leader who speaks on the power of belief. He is currently a national security analyst for Fox News. He co-wrote a policy paper entitled, "Choosing Victory: A Plan for Success in Iraq," which was the blueprint for America's successful surge in 2007.

Given his recent experience as a board member of a major insurance company, Keane was struck by the similarities between the military and our business. According to Keane, "The military, too, is a *value-based* organization." He considers the purpose of both organizations to be protecting others for the greater good. We in the financial services industry should focus on Keane's words to help overcome rejection. Imagine how strong your belief must be in the military, where people are not just dealing with rejection, but risking their lives!

It is vital to note that not all coming changes will be

negative. I'm sure you might have heard of Dan Sullivan, the founder of the Strategic Coach® program that serves entrepreneurs—many of them in the financial services area. He recently wrote *The Good That Financial Advisors Do*. Within this work he declared, "Being a financial advisor to upwardly mobile individuals in the 21st century is one of the most important roles in our society."[11]

That should make you feel pretty good, because here is the bigger paradigm that is emerging. The cultural, governmental, and corporate safety nets that people once enjoyed are in jeopardy. In 2011, we saw riots in the UK, Wisconsin, Greece, and France. In France, they wanted to shift the retirement age from 60 to 62. I personally have a retirement date, and it's two weeks before I die.

But that's the trap. Some people cannot wait to retire. They might be enriched, but they are certainly not fulfilled. If you really love what you do, why would you want to retire? If you are unfulfilled and miserable while you're working at 60, what do you think you'll be when you're retired at age 62? The same unfulfilled and miserable person in retirement. In life, it's not what you get; it's what you become. As Billy Joel said, "Either way, it's okay, you wake up with yourself." The other benefit our business provides is the ability to do something that's life sustaining. It's not enough to have a job that enriches you; it must also fulfill you. You should follow your true calling to help people rather than just taking the job to pay the bills.

---

[11] Dan Sullivan, *The Good That Financial Advisors Do* (Toronto: The Strategic Coach Inc., 2010).

We all recognize that people are living longer. There are no more safety nets. People are going to need someone in financial services—someone like you—to make it. I think the way our profession is perceived will dramatically change. Societies will figure out that it's cheaper to employ financial professionals who advise people than to give unfunded pensions to someone who is going to live another 30 years into retirement.

Once you believe that you're doing something significant, it is time to take action. Positive thinking doesn't always lead to positive action, but positive action *always* leads to positive thinking. Let me ask you a question. What is the worst part of this business? What do you dread the most? Nine out of ten people in financial services say, "Asking a stranger to see me and having the possibility of rejection." So, if we really believe that we have a significant purpose, then we have to make a commitment to that purpose. Here is my suggestion: Take that number one fear head on. Make a commitment to ask X number of people a day to see you. That's an actual "ask," not just a dial.

When I was selling, my number was seven. It could be 6:30 in the morning at the gym, and if I saw a guy lifting weights, I'd ask to see him. Even if he said no, that's one down, six to go. My thought process was: How many more can I get checked off my list before 10:00 in the morning? I turned it into a game. If I felt good one day, I might do a few more—say three—to know I had an easier next day in only having to contact four people. If you're new to the business, you should be asking at least 10 people a day to see you. If you're more established, you can get away with a few less. The key is this: If your goal was 10, and you got 10 NOs, you still had a successful day because you faced your fears. You know if you consistently ask at least 10 people a day, you'd likely build up appointments. On the other hand, if you ask 800 people to see you, and every person rejects you, you had better get to work on your telephone skills. To me, this isn't just a process or an exercise. It's a reaffirmation of faith — a faith that you do something worthwhile.

Saint Augustine once said, "Faith is to believe what you do not yet see; the reward for this faith is to see what you believe." I am not attempting to dive into a religious discussion with you, but I do think there is a spiritual side to the business. This is one business where you must have harmony between *who* you are and *what* you do.

The other paradigm this process facilitates is that you are managing to your effort and not to your results. You don't control your results. You cannot control whether someone will see you or whether someone will buy from you. Additionally, you cannot control underwriting decisions, the stock market, or interest rates. The only thing you can control is your effort. Ghandi said that true satisfaction does not come in the achievement, but in the effort. Total effort is total victory. The idea is to manage what you control, which is your effort. The more you prospect, the better you feel, and the more it reaffirms your significant purpose. This is how you can move yourself from motivation to inspiration.

There are three types of people in the world:
1. People who listen to your advice
2. People who don't listen to your advice
3. People who have never heard your advice

Your job is to keep the people who listen to your advice. Avoid the people who don't listen to it. Approach the people who haven't heard your advice and turn them into people who listen to your advice.

This process is the DNA of sales and profitability. Every financial organization wants to attain three goals:

1. Increase per rep productivity, which leads to increased rep retention

2. Manage the mix of business to diversify revenue streams

3. Create a client-centric culture that focuses on value, not price

These goals deal with the financial objectives of the enterprise. Many executives acknowledge that nothing happens until a sale is made, but I think this is shortsighted. I believe you have to start at the beginning. Not when a sale is made, but when a prospect is asked for an appointment. *That* is the beginning. If sales reps don't feel good about themselves, or are just in this business for the money, many will avoid the rejection of prospecting. This will decrease per rep productivity, and when reps can't make a living they will leave, lowering retention. People have told me,

"Joe, we really like when you talk about *Life of Significance*, but we need to focus on the business." But I find that if you don't start at the beginning, you may not have a business.

I instituted the daily contact commitment in the latter part of 2007. In 2010, my mentor, **Nick Murray**, published a book called *The Game of Numbers*. At one of his seminars, he was amazed to learn that his followers—major financial planning types—had stopped prospecting! He never considered writing a prospecting book because he thought his clientele was beyond it. Looks like we could all go back to the basics.

If you accept my challenge and establish a daily contact commitment, consistently asking a specific number of people a day to see you, you'll wind up having more real problems. Appointments will cancel, illustrations might be incomplete, and underwriting processes could go wrong. You will have more real problems, but no imaginary ones.

Try these exercises:

Make four lists of people you can put into circles of consideration:
1. *Close friends/relatives*
2. *Acquaintances*
3. *Colleagues in organizations*
4. *Others in your community (business owners, officials, professionals)*

Personalize the considerations for each person on your list by:
- *Work situation*
- *Family situation*
- *Life stage*
- *Special circumstances*

Think about how you can help address those considerations. Incorporate them into your daily contact commitment list.

One last point I want to make is that much emphasis is placed on goal setting, and rightfully so. Goals are important, but as I mentioned before, they have to sync up with your beliefs. Goals are the *what*; technique, knowledge, and skills are the *how*. But believing in your purpose—that you live a significant life in the service of others—is the *why*. Why you would practice this profession. The *why*, in my judgment, needs to transcend your own personal needs. The more global your recognition of *why* leads to greater inspiration, which gives you the courage to practice the *how* of the daily contact commitment. In turn, this reinforces that you continue on, allowing the process to give you the *what* that you seek.

Where did you learn your relationship skills?

What motivates you?

What makes you feel great at the end of a workday or at the end of a conversation with a client?

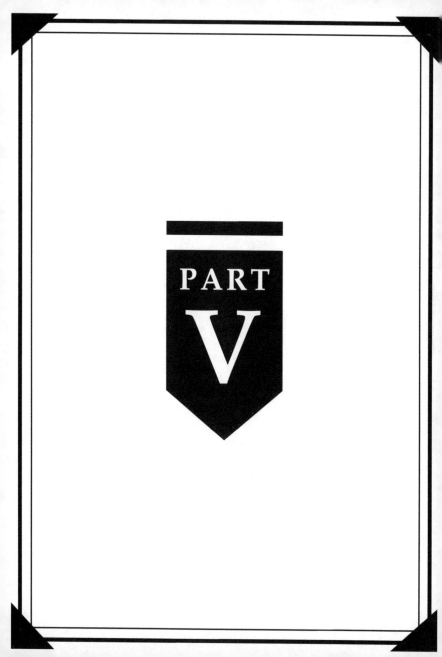

PART

V

CHAPTER 17

Your Life of Significance

"A hero is someone who has given his or her life to something bigger than oneself."

— JOSEPH CAMPBELL

Hero may seem like a big word, but in my presentations, I know I am speaking to heroes every day. I am writing this book for you, because you are a hero, too. We have captured hundreds of interviews with heroes who, just by doing their jobs, have changed lives and influenced generations to come. Advocating for a family's financial well-being is heroic because, using Campbell's definition, it is doing "something bigger than oneself." This is what you have chosen to do. By ensuring that individuals can protect their assets and their personal dignity, and by helping them to build a meaningful legacy, you will build your own legacy as well—one of quiet, heroic significance.

I would not have written this book if I did not believe that everyone can live a life of significance. Many people lead such lives but never realize the impact they've had on those around them and on generations to come. There are probably just as many people who miss the opportunity to live their lives as significantly as possible because they are out of touch with the signals around them. Certain practices would help them become more in tune with those signals. Few professions offer the potential to establish such a legacy of significance.

Living a life of significance begins with the impact you can have on the lives of your clients. I can think of no other profession that can provide clients with protection, independence, dignity, and legacy. Living a Life of Significance isn't just my story — it's your story, too.

If nothing else, when you finish reading this book, I want you to be proud and enthusiastic about what you do. It may help if you make some comparisons with professions that are commonly held in high esteem. Consider physicians. In a way, they fail in the end, because everyone dies. With the help you provide, generation after generation will live on — as Chief Seattle eloquently put it — through the web of life.

A life of significance focuses on the protection of others. The preservation of human dignity is something bigger than yourself, and ultimately involves building a meaningful legacy of your own. At the beginning of this book, I said that not every journey looks the same. At the same time, every journey truly does have a story to tell.

From my experience, I can offer the following suggestions:

- *Question early and often.*
- *Exercise both sides of your brain.*
- *Be disciplined. Make a daily contact commitment.*
- *Create a celebratory culture.*
- *Make a commitment — both to your clients and prospecting.*
- *Trust that you can live a life of significance from where you are right now.*

CHAPTER 18

Question Early & Often

Throughout this book, I have encouraged you to question things around you and within yourself. The types of questions I've included and continued in this chapter are intended to keep your senses sharpened. I want to better equip you for recognizing and responding to situations for yourself and the clients you serve. Consider this analogy:

> In New York, building maintenance is a huge business. One facet of this business involves a meticulous process of tapping on the bricks or stones of a building's façade to ensure that each one is solidly in place. If you don't tap the stones, you run the risk of one coming loose and falling onto a busy sidewalk below. The risk is greater if the loose stone is a keystone, because in that case, a structural collapse is possible. Tapping away at your own façade can ensure that your foundations are strong.
>
> Questions are the way to sound out the potential weaknesses in your self-understanding and your knowledge of your surroundings. Remember, you are in good company when you question something about your life every day.

As a result, you may avoid the day when you find that you are far from where you intended to be.

You should stay awake to the world around you and the world inside you. Make sure that you have an idea where you are and how you fit into the situation. As an insurance professional, you will often find yourself viewing a situation a bit differently than someone else might. For example, when you go to a barbecue with friends and family, you may see kids there who wouldn't be present if one or the other of their parents couldn't bring them. Others might shake off that realization as a maudlin distraction. Unlike other people, you have it in your power to help someone potentially prevent that situation.

Your first step in this process is to give yourself permission to entertain questions about your general life, your choices, and your career path. If you are comfortable with questions, you have already stepped off of square one.

If you need more encouragement to begin questioning, you can review the stories shared in earlier chapters and read the vignettes to follow.

Paris Lewis, a financial advisor, questioned whether a client had the right coverage.

> *When he first met with this client (let's call him Jim), Paris knew he wasn't Jim's first insurance agent. Jim had a 30-year-old policy already in force. Paris questioned, in his own mind from that very*

first meeting, whether this policy was sufficient for Jim. However, he let Jim set the pace. Jim went slowly at first, simply asking for a beneficiary change. Paris handled it quickly and efficiently. Jim then asked him to handle a few more administrative details. Before long, Jim asked Paris to become his financial advisor and shared his full financial situation with Paris, a professional he had come to trust. Paris revisited Jim's life insurance coverage and reviewed other protection and investment options available to his client.

A few years later, Jim called Paris and asked him to stop by, "as a friend, not a financial advisor." Jim revealed that he had been diagnosed with Lou Gehrig's disease, a progressive, incurable, and ultimately fatal condition. Paris found his mind racing. Had he considered everything his friend would need to protect his income? To continue a life with dignity and independence? To leave a legacy for his family? Thankfully, Paris could answer "Yes." He continues to serve Jim's family — his children, widow, siblings, and now his grandchildren — as a trusted financial advisor. To them, Paris is a hero.

Lonnie Colson, a financial advisor, questioned a client's assessment of his own needs.

Lonnie's client — we'll call him Frank — came to Lonnie knowing exactly what he needed, or so he thought. Frank was 30 years old, with a wife and two young boys. They had just purchased a home, and Frank wanted mortgage insurance. Lonnie questioned the narrowness of Frank's request. He ran a full analysis and spoke to Frank honestly. He asked about Frank's income and educational needs, knowing these factors were just as deserving of consideration as his house payments were if anything were to happen to him. Frank agreed that he had missed the big picture, until Lonnie put things into perspective from his family's point of view.

Two months later, Frank's two sons ran out to meet Lonnie as he came up their driveway. In the way that only children can, they confided, "You know, our Daddy isn't coming home anymore." Lonnie did know. He was there to deliver the benefit check to Frank's widow. Frank had been killed in a car accident earlier that week.

Maybe the polite thing for Lonnie to have done two months prior would've been to nod and tell Frank that mortgage insurance was a great idea. Maybe it would have made Frank feel smart for "knowing" exactly what he needed. But it wouldn't have protected his family. Lonnie knew that his job was to protect that family, not to fill an order like at a fast-food restaurant. Lonnie knew the significance

> *of considering the big picture. He spoke for those who couldn't speak for themselves — Frank's sons and now widow — and helped his clients see what they really needed. Those two boys went straight to college from the home that their father had protected.*

As you can tell from these stories, I am not promoting a particular sales approach. Each of these individuals built a relationship in a different way. The point is that they built a relationship. As a result, both their clients' lives and their own lives were enriched.

If you are ready to consider some of the important questions in your own life, you can start with these:

1. What situations challenge you most (e.g., cold calls, closing, public speaking)?

2. What inspired you to pursue the field of insurance?

3. Do you have any questions that you didn't have when you started reading this book?

4. What would a life of significance look like to you?

It may help to think of people you consider to have lived, or currently be living these kinds of lives.

As you work through these questions, you may find that they lead to other questions. That would actually be an excellent outcome. You might want to consider an ongoing practice of revisiting these questions.

CHAPTER 19
The Most Important Question

There is no more important question than whether the recommendation you make to a client is the one that you consider the best choice for that client. As a seasoned professional, I can tell you that you'll have greater and more meaningful success when you operate ethically. This is not a philosophical position; it has tangible financial implications.

A 2006 securities industry study found that firms in the securities industry are spending 13.1% of net revenue on compliance-related activities. In other words, as an industry, these firms are spending at least $25.5 billion a year on compliance-related activities. Regulatory and legislative mandates on compliance-related spending resulted in major increases for 92.1% of the firms surveyed. These same mandates translated to an increase in the time devoted to compliance since 2002 for 97.2% of the firms surveyed. Average capital expenditures per firm on compliance is $3.9 million dollars, which represents an average increase of 366.1% since 2002.[12]

These trends have an important connection to living a life of significance because compliance is directly related to ethical selling. Nothing is more vital in the financial industry than maintaining client confidence and abiding within the

[12] "The Cost of Compliance in the US Securities Industry," Survey Report, Securities Industry Association, February 2006.

regulatory and legislative mandates established to protect consumers. A life of significance is one of ethical behavior. As companies continue to devote an enormous amount of time, money, and attention to compliance, they will place even greater value on the financial professionals who continually do the right thing for their clients. Companies understand that when it comes to compliance, an ounce of prevention is worth a pound of cure.

The heart of ethical selling is in understanding that we don't just sell products, we advocate for our clients and those who depend upon them. This moral obligation can differentiate you from purely profit-motivated competitors in ways you may not expect. It can provide a sustainable advantage, as your solutions bear out the message you use to sell them over time.

CHAPTER 20

Exercise Both Sides of Your Brain

In the financial services industry, the most valuable resource that producers have is their ability to connect with people. This means understanding the difference between left-brain and right-brain concepts:

- The left brain thinks; the right brain feels.
- The left brain communicates; the right brain connects.
- The left brain knows; the right brain believes.

Daniel Pink warns us in his book *A Whole New Mind* that intuition should not be underestimated in any profession.[13] It is not a matter of intellect over emotion, but a combination of emotional and rational intelligence that positions people for success. In the business of insurance, emotional intelligence is a core competency. It may also be the key to regaining a sense of self-worth and a real enthusiasm for the valuable service you provide.

Science and sociology correspond in the idea that you should value both intelligence and intuition. Now economists are following suit. In the insurance business, you will want to respect both of these attributes in your clients as well.

[13] Pink, *A Whole New Mind*.

Measuring Success: Mike Amine's Story

One agent's story can serve as a reminder that you should approach your contacts with their best interest in mind and not your own. There are times when you may be too close to a situation to realize you aren't seeing the person's needs clearly. Read Mike's story to comprehend what I mean.

> *As a young man starting out fresh in this business, I was always measuring my own success. We have so many ways to do that. There are awards, achievements — all types of recognition to strive for — and these are all worthy goals. I remember that hitting those targets loomed heavily in my mind on the day I went to my parents' house to talk to my dad about a life policy. I was very clear that he needed the protection in place to ensure that my mom would be taken care of if anything happened to him. My dad absolutely agreed.*
>
> *As we worked out the details around the kitchen table, my mom said, "Mike, I'd like you to write a policy for me, too. I want to have life insurance." It was so sweet. But I said, "No, Mom. You don't need life insurance. Nothing's ever going to happen to you." We laughed. And she smiled at me and let it go.*

My wife and I were on vacation the next summer when my brother called. "I've got some bad news," he said. "Mom's been diagnosed with ovarian cancer." I dropped the phone. My wife had to pick it up and finish the conversation for me. She told me as gently as she could that things did not look good. Within a year, my mother died from the cancer.

We never spoke about it, but I knew that I had taken away her chance to leave the legacy she wanted to leave. If I had only listened to my mom. She taught me an invaluable lesson. You see, in my mind, I didn't need to sell my mom a policy that day a year back. I was on track to do the level of business that I needed to achieve the success I was looking for that year. I didn't need that extra premium. No, but she needed it. And I was so focused on my own goals that I denied it to her.

I measure success very differently now; I hear my mother's voice loud and clear. Awards are great, but they come second to the vital part of this business. What we do is immeasurably significant. We give people that chance to leave a legacy, to live with dignity, to give something to their loved ones at the most difficult time they will ever face. Because I didn't listen to my mother, her voice echoes in my ear. I will never make that mistake again. I hear you, Mom.

CHAPTER 21

Trust Yourself

"Is the system going to flatten you out and deny you your humanity, or are you going to be able to make use of the system to the attainment of human purposes?"

— JOSEPH CAMPBELL

I will reiterate my belief that everyone can live a life of significance. By this point in the book, you may be thinking that the profession you are in can lead you toward this kind of life. I cannot think of many professions, especially in the financial services arena, that offer such an opportunity to change lives and influence future generations in a way that will ensure a meaningful legacy.

I have stayed on course with my internal compass in many respects. I have changed jobs, and I have changed companies. Other times, I found a way to endure in the same company and maintain my course, working to change things from within. I would encourage you to understand that you don't have to leave your job or change your profession to achieve a life of significance. If you are in the insurance business, I am fully confident that you can live such a life. In fact, you probably already do.

Last Wish

As our business grows and changes, our reach has become increasingly global. Our ability to touch lives now extends across all seven continents. The story of one agent and her Chinese client gives a view of this worldwide connection and its immeasurable value to clients around the globe.

> *Ying Ling Zhang's story is one that not only shows how service can reach around the world, but also how personally clients come to value those who help them make the right decisions in life. Ying Ling tells of a client who bought a policy at the beginning of one summer and was diagnosed with cervical cancer the following June. The client called Ying Ling to tell her about the first surgery, and soon after said that she did not have much time to live. She wanted to go home to China to be with her aging mother for the remainder of her time.*
>
> *Ying Ling assured her that everything would be taken care of at home. She then set the necessary process in motion to ensure that, though her client's treatments were nearly $1,000 per day, the checks would be there to cover her care.*
>
> *As she neared the end of her life, Ying Ling's client asked her husband to call Ying Ling and thank her. Although she could no longer speak, she wanted Ying Ling to know that she was "the person I want to*

> *thank most on earth. I will pray for her from heaven."*
> *Ying Ling tells this incredibly moving story with striking humility. "It was [my client] who made the right decision," Ying Ling says humbly.*

Of course, this is true; none of us can force a client to make a decision. But Ying Ling clearly made a tremendous difference in her client's life — in her quality of life, her independence to travel thousands of miles for her final days, and the dignity of dying in the way she wanted. Ying Ling's story represents a life of significance on a global scale.

Tell me another profession that could have had such a profound effect on a complete stranger. Can you imagine that the last person this woman thanked before she died was Ying Ling? Let me assure you that you do not experience that kind of intense human interaction when you beat the S&P by 7 basis points for 3 months.

Some people think that our purpose is to find meaning in life. I don't think that's what we seek. What we seek is to experience being alive. Viktor Frankl wrote, "Success, like happiness, cannot be pursued; it must ensue, and it only does so as the unintended side effect of one's personal dedication to a cause greater than oneself, or as the by-product of one's surrender to a person other than oneself."[14] The bottom line is that you can't live a significant life without helping others. Those in financial services do it for a living, but how often do they dwell on it?

[14] Viktor Frankl, *Man's Search for Meaning* (Boston: Beacon Press, 1959).

It's important to remember that all the hard work, intelligence, and emotional commitment in the world cannot guarantee that every client will make the best decisions. Rejection is a common occurrence in our business. There will always be clients who cannot "get out of their own way." In those situations, we can learn new lessons to apply another time, but we cannot fall into the trap of allowing our own self-esteem to be tied to the results.

Roland Basinski shared one such story with me.

I had a client who was about to retire. He called me up to say that he was letting his whole life policies lapse. He just couldn't see his way clear to keep up the premiums. These policies totaled $500,000. I took the opportunity to get together with my client and talk about the importance of maintaining that coverage, especially since Social Security was the only other buffer he and his wife had. He was resolute on the topic. All he could think of was the money going out.

Sure enough, he let the policies lapse. He died soon afterward, leaving his wife with only the Social Security to live on. I was heartbroken, but I knew that I had done my best to convince him to keep the policies current.

What I took away from this experience is a greater awareness that I should touch base with my clients —

even when they're covered and they seem to be doing fine. If I had asked him 10 years earlier, maybe I could have helped him avoid his flustered reaction. Hopefully, I can help my other clients get out in front of their retirement choices.

CHAPTER 22

Personal Journey

You have your own personal journey ahead of you, as a financial professional and as a person; seldom does a profession allow you success in both. As I have revealed, the mother-in-law PSA I saw in 1999 caused me to think about the impact life insurance would have had on my family. Up until that point, I never spoke of my personal situation. I fell into a trap of separating who I was from what I did. This absence of balance is widespread in the West, leading to situations like the one in France, where people cannot wait to retire.

I spoke of my anger on the main platform at the MDRT conference in 2004. For the first time, I personalized the business I had been in for 30 years. I shared how Joseph Campbell's connection to Chief Seattle revealed a culture and a way of thinking that did not compartmentalize life. It is in the synchronization of what you do and who you are that assists in your transformation.

The incident that finally completed my transformation was a meeting at MetLife. Despite a 23-year career in the home office of MetLife, I was never a terribly popular figure. You see, they ran a lot of meetings. You know the definition of a meeting, don't you? It's the unfit managing the unwilling to do the unnecessary. After the meeting started, one of the participants attacked me. The person said, "He's not a team player. He always demands what he wants, and he hurts my feelings!" I have heard this throughout my life. I never gave it much credence, and I thought the other person had a problem. But I said to myself, "You've heard this a lot, and maybe there's something to it." I always had a fire in my belly, but I never answered the question: WHY did I do what I did?

And with this I continued questioning: How did I get into this business? Why is it I am speaking to tens of thousands of people around the world every year? How did this happen? The answer came to me in an instant.

I feel that I have been directed by my mother to get where I am today. As Joseph Campbell would say, the way I "follow my bliss" is to talk to the thousands who can save millions from a fate like the one she endured.

For the first time in my life, *who* and *what* I did were in congruence. I understood my purpose; my life had meaning. In life it is not the pain of the journey, but the rapture of the revelation. That which I thought was a tragedy was a triumph. You all have your very own personal journeys, but there are very few professions where you can make a very good living and also fulfill your obligations to others. Success is getting what you want; happiness is wanting what you get. But I'll tell you the best thing that happened.

I'm Irish, and my mother always wanted to go home to Ireland. She never made it. But in 2006, my MDRT buddy **Brendan Glennon** invited me to speak at the MDRT meeting in Dublin. I told my mother's story and showed her picture. In my mind, I took my mother home. This was a defining moment, a significant experience that ultimately brought my journey in life full circle.

WHAT PEOPLE ARE SAYING

"Joe Jordan's engaging stories will help any advisor deepen their sense of meaning and purpose by reminding them of the significant and profound value they are uniquely positioned to create in the world. *Living a Life of Significance* is a gift to any advisor who wants a boost in energy, confidence, and clarity about how their work creates profound positive transformations in countless lives."

Dan Sullivan
Founder of Strategic Coach®

"I see Joe's unique abilities in the contrast he presents in his words, philosophy, and appearance. Joe's penetrating voice, deep in conviction and passion, tells stories through metaphors, poetry, and folklore—drawing the listener in so as to understand his message. His philosophy became self-evident as he understood how certain financial tools would have changed his family's life. His appearance conveys uniqueness and confidence; a rugby player with soft hands, Joe looks like he could quell a small war and propose a touching toast in the same venue. This is a man so comfortable in who he is and where he is going that he can wear spats into L.L. Bean with ease, so that people are curious to know more about him. Joe has an air of wisdom, empathy, and renaissance. All the best my friend."

Phil Harriman
Former MDRT President

"This book is a must-read. All organizations and individuals must have strong values. Joe Jordan focuses on these values. Although he talks about financial services, he is really talking about life."

Jack Keane
Retired Four-Star General & Former Vice Chief of Staff of the U.S. Army

"There are only a small handful of people in this world who go about their everyday life working to make a difference, and Joe is one of them. He can touch you like no one else. He makes you feel special and awakens you, so you have no choice but to step up and live your own personalized life of significance. The amazing thing is that whether you're in Kolkata, Manila, Buenos Aires, or Glasgow, Joe's words enter your being. *Living a Life of Significance* is something we all must choose to do, and Joe supplies the motivation."

Gordon Watson
Executive Vice President & Regional Managing Director, AIA Group

"Jordan is an Olympic-sized thinker who motivates and inspires in a manner that is without peer. Your practice has been short-changed if you haven't read every word."

Dr. Larry Barton, CAP®
President and CEO, The American College

"*Living a Life of Significance* is essential reading for your practice and your soul."

Nick Murray
"Resources" in Nick Murray Interactive, July 2011

"Joe is an inspirational speaker who cares passionately about the financial profession and fully understands the challenges these experts face."

Fay Goddard, UK
Chief Executive of The Personal Finance Society

ABOUT THE AUTHOR

Joseph W. Jordan began his career with Home Life Insurance Company in 1974. He was "Rookie of the Year" and a member of the Million Dollar Round Table (MDRT). Directly after running insurance sales at PaineWebber from 1981 to 1988, he joined MetLife to build its annuity business. Later he was responsible for all retail product development at MetLife, initiating fee-based financial planning. Joe founded the Behavioral Finance Organization at MetLife.

Joe has been on the North American MDRT main platform in 2004 and on the main platform of multiple MDRT experiences around the world. Jordan spoke at the 2011 Retirement Summit in Monte Carlo and was the keynote speaker at the 2012 Life Insurance and Market Research Association (LIMRA) Conference in Hong Kong. He was the chairman of the Personal Finance Society (PFS) conference in Birmingham, UK, and is the founder of the Retirement Institute, formally known as the National Association for Variable Annuities (NAVA).

Joe is an independent consultant, author, an international speaker. In 2011 Mr. Jordan released the first edition of this book, *Living a Life of Significance*, which was listed as one of the top five books of 2011 by *Financial Advisor* Magazine. In May of 2012 he was featured in the cover story of *Life Insurance Selling* as one of the legends of the industry. Additionally, Joe has been named one of the "Top Irish Americans on Wall Street" for three years in a row.

Joe is a member of the Fordham University Football Hall of Fame and played rugby for the New York Athletic Club for over 30 years.